GOLDWATER

GOLDWATER

A Tribute to a Twentieth-Century Political Icon

BILL RENTSCHLER

Foreword by Senator John McCain

CONTEMPORARY BOOKS

Library of Congress Cataloging-in-Publication Data

Rentschler, Bill.
   Goldwater : a tribute to a twentieth-century political icon / Bill
Rentschler ; foreword by John McCain.
      p.   cm.
   Includes index.
   ISBN 0-8092-9556-3
   1. Goldwater, Barry M. (Barry Morris, 1909–98).
2. Goldwater, Barry M. (Barry Morris, 1909–98)—Political and
social views.   3. United States. Congress. Senate—
Biography.   4. Legislators—United States—Biography.
5. Conservatism—United States—History—20th century.
6. United States—Politics and government—1945–1989.
E748.G64   2000
n-us—dc21   00-55557
                                                       CIP

Unless otherwise specified, all photos are courtesy of the Arizona
Historical Foundation, University Libraries, ASU.

Interior design by Nick Panos

Published by Contemporary Books
A division of NTC/Contemporary Publishing Group, Inc.
4255 West Touhy Avenue
Lincolnwood (Chicago), Illinois 60712-1975 U.S.A.
Printed in the United States of America
International Standard Book Number: 0-8092-9556-3
00   01   02   03   04   05   LB   14   13   12   11   10   9   8   7   6   5   4   3   2   1

The brief span of two years beginning with the death of Barry Goldwater on May 29, 1998, was for me "the worst of times."

In that period, my two younger brothers, my only siblings, and too many dear friends completed their earthly missions.

To them I dedicate this book.

Peter Robert Rentschler
James Peter Rentschler
William Benjamin Davies
Jack Hoogasian
Allan Marshall Marin
Dennis Sheehan
Jeanne Hurley Simon
James Leslie Zacharias
David Bell Peck III

Contents

FOREWORD

Barry Goldwater put his country and our founding ideals before himself, and we never had a better champion. He believed we all have a duty to the country, a concept that once was as common to our political lexicon as "sound bite" and "spin control" are today. And he performed his duty magnificently—tirelessly, forcefully, effectively, and with a style as honest and wide open as the state he loved so dearly.

The best thing that can ever be said of anyone is that they served a cause greater than their self-interest. All the well-earned testimonials and accolades to Barry Goldwater that filled the nation's newspapers and airwaves after his death can be summed up in that one tribute: He served a cause greater than his self-interest.

I hope and pray I can measure up to that standard set over many years by the great and singular man who held this Senate seat before me.

American politics is awash in pledges today: pledges to cut taxes; to soak the rich; to create wealth; to redistribute wealth; to end welfare; to feed the hungry, clothe the naked, and shelter the homeless; to fight for the middle class, the working class, the underclass, and the entrepreneurial class.

Barry Goldwater served America, all of America, a country conceived in liberty, a country that let you pledge any damn thing you wanted as long as it didn't cost someone else their liberty. He served freedom—a cause greater than, but encompassing, his self-interest—and to that cause he pledged, as a famous group of East Coast radicals once pledged, his life, his fortune, and his sacred honor.

As I experienced the exhilaration and uplift—along with the harsh blows and deep trauma—of my presidential test, I have taken comfort, sustenance, and example from Barry's rare courage and candor. I have gone forward devoted to his undiluted passion for liberty and justice for all our citizens, which he and I consider the inviolate underpinnings of a free society.

He once wrote that he was "better equipped to be a military officer than a politician. There's no greater service to this country than the defense of its freedom." But he was mistaken about that.

He was a superb military officer, but he was also an extraordinarily gifted politician. That he was an unusually open, honest, and no-nonsense politician did not make him unsuited for the profession, only uncommon.

In uniform and in politics, Barry's purpose was always the defense of freedom, and nobody, before or since, managed the task more ably or more colorfully than Barry Goldwater.

He held his principles close to his heart, where he held his love of country. He lived his public life and his private life according to the dictates of his principles, and woe to the miscreant who ran afoul of them, whether it be a communist superpower or a colleague who trimmed his sails according to the passing whims of public opinion. Barry always rushed to defend his ground, whether the ground he defended was in fashion at the time or not.

He defended freedom in all its manifestations because he appreciated what freedom conferred on America—the distinction of being the last, best hope of humanity, the haven and advocate for all who believed in the God-given dignity of the human being. He loved America because freedom is her honor. And, as a young man and an old one, he took risks for his country's honor.

He never shrank from the call of his conscience, from the call of duty. He gave honorable service in wartime and never mustered out in peacetime, serving for many long years in his beloved Air Force Reserve.

In politics, a profession he loved despite his frequent frank assessments of its less admirable practitioners, he risked his career to give the country "a choice, not an echo." No one knew better than Barry that he was unlikely to win the presidency in 1964. But he felt the Republican Party and the country needed some straight talk about old values, and he figured he was the man to give it to them the loudest. So he did, knowing the slings and arrows he would suffer, but confident that his course was honorable. And he ended that campaign, as he ended his political career twenty-two years later, with his personal integrity unblemished, his honor unassailable.

Barry's outspoken defense of liberty at home was equaled by the care he took in protecting our security abroad. Perhaps his most lasting legislative achievement in a Senate career notable for many achievements was the Goldwater-Nickles Defense Reorganization Act.

Only Barry had the stature and resolve to undertake the systemic reform of the military. And, as we observed in the splendid performance of our military in the Persian Gulf War, notably free of the chain-of-command and service rivalry problems of the past, and saw the extraordinary effectiveness of their weapons, from the Patriot missile to the M1 tank, we witnessed the great contribution that Barry Goldwater made to our defense. It is no exaggeration to say that today's American armed forces, which have no equal in the world, are the armed forces Barry Goldwater created.

As I've observed on several occasions, I am both blessed and burdened to have succeeded Barry Goldwater to the United States Senate. I am blessed by the honor of it but burdened by the certain knowledge that long after I have left public office, Americans will still celebrate the contributions Barry Goldwater made to their well-being, while I and my successors will enjoy much less notable reputations.

I came to Arizona in midlife. Barry was here before Arizona was a state. He was her favorite son, and always will be, because the people of this blessed place knew, as sure as they knew anything, that Barry Goldwater was one of them. He once broke down in an interview while describing his deep affection for Arizona. "Arizona is 113,900 square miles of heaven that God cut out," he said as he fought back tears. "I love it so much."

Barry Goldwater will always be *the* senator from Arizona, the one history recalls with appreciation and delight. In all the histories of American politics, he will remain a chapter unto himself. The rest of us will have to make do as footnotes.

—SENATOR JOHN MCCAIN

PREFACE

"There will never be another Barry Goldwater," Nancy Reagan wrote me recently, sharing her own thoughts as well as those of her ailing husband.

Barry was truly one of a kind, a singular senator and human being who can't be compared to others who served beside him, before him, or after him in the "world's most exclusive club," or in the presidency during his lifetime.

Barry was his own man, unbent by the stiff winds of controversy that often swirled about him. He was a stout oak who stood firm against all manner of sound and fury. He lived all but eleven years of a century that historian Arthur Schlesinger Jr. described as "this disordered, disheveled, fantastic, path-breaking century, this crazy epoch of troubles and tragedies and triumphs." And Barry Goldwater lived most every day to the hilt.

His brother Bob, brisk and staunch at ninety, told me in early 2000, "Barry was the most honest man I ever knew." Scoff if you will at the source, but how many people would say that with a straight face about a sibling? "We were always very close," Bob said of Barry, along with baby sister Carolyn, who died in June 1999, and himself. All three lived deep into their ninth decade.

Barry was genuinely loved and respected even by his most virulent philosophical antagonists.

A perfect example is Senator Edward M. (Ted) Kennedy, an ardent liberal, who wrote on Goldwater's death, "I inherited my friendship and affection for Barry from my brothers. They knew him and liked him and respected him in the Senate, and so did I. We often disagreed, but our friendship far transcended any disagreement."

Ted Kennedy repeated President John F. Kennedy's comment shortly before his benumbing assassination in 1963: "I really like Barry," said JFK. "And if he's the Republican nominee and I'm licked, at least it will be on the issues. At least people will have a clear choice."

During his long life span, Barry never received his full due, mainly because of the savage misrepresentations spread widely in the presidential campaign of 1964 by Lyndon Johnson and his coterie, by the "eastern liberal" clique within his own Republican Party, and by an overwhelmingly hostile media wolf pack.

Goldwater said to me at one point almost matter-of-factly, "I was depicted as a grotesque public monster. Hell, if half the things they said about me were true, I'd never have voted for myself."

These attacks have faded, but they have lingered, too, in bits and pieces, and they have served to misrepresent this good man to this day.

As the twentieth century wound down, and the nation was caught up in the hype for "the new millennium," we were beset everywhere by endless lists—lists of the top hundred sports figures, foremost media stars, legendary entertainers, influential political figures, on and on, ad nauseam, mostly compiled by youthful "experts" whose recall extended back perhaps ten or, at most, twenty years.

Nowhere on those lists was the name of Barry Goldwater to be found, even though he lived for nine eventful decades of the century, served thirty visible years in the U.S. Senate, became the choice of a major political party as its presidential standard-bearer, and stood as the acknowledged godfather of the dominant conservative movement that persists and gathers strength today.

This testifies not only to the superficiality of those ubiquitous lists but also to the savagery of the assaults on Goldwater during that 1964 campaign.

His undiluted "authenticity" was trampled by the obscene excess of his foes.

In fact, Goldwater's trademark authenticity and straight talk were used against him with devastating impact to create a reckless, unsavory, extremist caricature. His foes would stop at nothing in their zeal to convince the electorate that Barry Goldwater as president would unleash atomic weapons, dismantle Social Security, and run a repressive, racist administration. It was sinfully untrue, but it worked.

In political cravings uncovered by current polls in the presidential race of 2000, voters are looking for "authenticity" in the candidates they favor. Americans today—those who care and pay attention—want public officials who are authentic: truthful and candid, mature, levelheaded, even somewhat straitlaced. That was Barry Goldwater, and there are precious few of his cut on the scene today.

Rather, we are drowning in blow-dried, skin-deep, painfully narrow, guru-driven, sophomoric types who feed the cynicism and doubts of ordinary people.

Probable voters seemed to find that quality of authenticity in the challengers—former Senator Bill Bradley and especially John McCain, Goldwater's successor in the Senate—to a greater degree than in Texas Governor George W. Bush and Vice President Al Gore.

But no candidate in the past half century could wear the badge of "authentic" with greater authority than Barry Goldwater. This may be yet another dimension of his legacy.

If you knew Barry Goldwater—really knew him—you couldn't help liking him. He was a charmer without making the slightest attempt to charm. He was fun to be around, easygoing, but committed defiantly to the principles he held sacred—mainly individual liberty and equal justice, which were the hallmarks of "his" conservatism. He had a knack for making you feel comfortable in his presence. He had a marvelous sense of humor and could poke fun at himself with the deft self-deprecating touch of his good friend Jack

Kennedy. He was intensely loyal, though when it came to running his presidential campaign, he abandoned his philosophical allies in favor of loyalty to the "Arizona mafia," with whom he had longer and deeper ties. This probably was due in part to his "insecurity" in testing the waters nationally for the only time.

I first met Barry in the late 1950s as I was getting active in politics and shortly before I lost a tight, disappointing, issue-oriented race for the U.S. Senate in the Republican primary of 1960. In 1964, I became an elected Goldwater delegate from Illinois and was said to be the youngest in the nation. We stayed in touch ever since, through periodic visits, correspondence, and phone talks.

I do not claim to be an intimate or crony of Barry Goldwater, just a good friend whom he trusted to tell the truth, which is the most a good journalist can ask. He answered every question I ever asked him candidly and never with evasion.

These few snatches from some of the notes and letters he wrote me during the '90s speak to the nature of our friendship:

"It was good news to hear that you might be coming out to Scottsdale for a visit. I would love to see you. . . . I'm looking forward to it." (4/22/94)

"It was nice to receive your letter and look at those pictures. What handsome devils we were in 1964. . . ." (12/19/96, after his first mild stroke)

"By a very peculiar, and wonderful coincidence, the other night in bed, I picked up your book from my library, and read it again. Lo and behold in a couple of days, I get a letter from you." (12/30/92)

"I enjoyed what you wrote about me very much. It's typical Rentschler, and I guess it's typical Goldwater. However, Bill, I'm going to stay the way I've been all my life. Even though I haven't got a hell of a lot of years left, I'm going to have fun living them." (8/15/94)

While Barry was not an intellectual in the academic sense, he had a fine mind and a rare capacity to translate the most complex ideas into down-to-earth prose free of jargon and pomposity.

His smart, charming widow, Susan, spoke to me recently from Paradise Valley, where they lived, of his "instinctive intuition, which usually was right," and his uncanny ability to "size things up quickly and accurately."

I am convinced Susan gave him succor and love when he needed it most, in the final years, and gave him a kick in the tail when he was feeling depressed and sorry for himself. She was often accused by hardline conservatives of luring him away from bedrock rightist dogma. I seriously doubt it. While her heroes, she told me, were Eleanor Roosevelt and Adlai Stevenson (along with Churchill and Albert Einstein), she made it clear that Barry was ever his own man, who could not be swayed from his beliefs by her or anybody else. That rings true to anyone who knew Barry. It also testifies to the fact that he was never frozen into pure ideology, but adapted his long-held principles to the changing world around him.

I feel fortunate to have known this self-effacing giant of a man. I hope this small book will portray for those who read it some sense of the "real" Barry Goldwater. It is by no stretch a full-fledged biography or academic treatise but rather a more personal memoir intended to "flesh out" the "real" Barry Goldwater through a collection of reminiscences, anecdotes, intimate glimpses, and candid comments by him and others. It is a true story told by one who knew Barry, with heaviest reliance on the senator's own words, bedrock principles, and feelings. There is also my take on this simple, straightforward man, an American icon of integrity I greatly respected and genuinely liked as a human being and valued friend. I have attempted to depict the true Barry Goldwater in contrast to the distorted cardboard caricature that emerged from the 1964 coronation of LBJ.

Barry Goldwater may seem to some as far removed from today as the shaggy mammoths of prehistoric times. Probably no American so critical to the history of our times has been so thoroughly misrepresented by the mass media, the gullible public, and some of his political peers in both parties. What he said to the very end is in the Goldwater mold: Do what you believe, and let the chips fall. Follow your conscience ahead of old partisan loyalties, even if you make some people mad.

Barry is only a misty presence to many people questing and struggling, coping and floundering in today's America, oblivious to their precious gift of freedom. Few people of this time and place will understand. Perhaps because his agenda, his notion of public service, were as guileless and unbending as those of a lonesome cowboy from a distant, simpler past.

Only a few are left in American politics like Barry Goldwater. The polls didn't move him. He detested phonies. He derided high-priced political mercenaries. He sniffed at many of the slick trappings on today's campaign trail. He worried about the pernicious impact of money on the democratic process.

From my encounters with him over the years, I'm persuaded his measure of each big issue was not rooted in ideology, but simply what he concluded was best for his beloved country.

My wish is that this book will separate fact from outright falsehoods, half-truths, and scalding innuendo, and present a fair, more or less objective, but affectionate, portrait of this American original, whose love of country—"with liberty and justice for all"—transcended all else.

Acknowledgments

My first and foremost acknowledgment goes to Barry Goldwater himself, who in our conversations and correspondence was unfailingly candid in what he told me, and revealing of himself. Much of this book comes straight from the mind, heart, and pen of Barry. He answered every question without pause or equivocation. He offered suggestions that were helpful but not self-serving. His two autobiographies were excellent sources of his own words on a range of matters and issues and personal feelings. This book is essentially a tribute to and reflection of the "real" Barry.

Many people have contributed, provided valuable insights and personal reflections, and helped me immeasurably in a variety of ways.

Susan Wechsler Goldwater, Barry's fiercely supportive, no-nonsense second wife since early 1992, was incredibly generous, welcoming, and trusting. She gave me the run of their home. She also has given her intimate insights and personal photos for this book. Barry's brother, Bob—a close sibling for almost ninety years—was a fount of fond recollections and marvelous tales at once poignant, funny, and insightful. Other family members who contributed were Barry Jr. and Ray Prescott Johnson, nephew of Peggy Johnson, Barry's first wife.

My deep thanks go to those estimable persons who knew Barry in the political realm and provided me with their personal comments. These include three past presidents—Gerald Ford, Jimmy Carter, and George Bush—as well as colleagues from his Senate days, among them Bob Dole, Chuck Percy, Paul Simon, Bill Bradley, Ted Kennedy, Mark Hatfield, and Sam Nunn. Others who shared their personal views were Nancy Reagan, Walter Cronkite, Bill Buckley, Don Rumsfeld, and Bruce DuMont. Joanne Drake, President Reagan's chief of staff, assisted with the Reagans' comments.

I am greatly indebted to Senator John McCain, who has occupied Barry's Senate seat since his retirement in 1987, for his moving foreword to this book, and to his aides, Chief of Staff Mark Salter, Larry Pike in the Phoenix office, and Amy Alderson. My thanks, too, to First Lady Hillary Rodham Clinton, a "Goldwater Girl" from Illinois in 1964, for her warm words of "farewell."

My children, Sarah, Peter, Mary Alley, Phoebe Cole, and Hope (soon to be Hope Garbo)—from various points of the compass—prodded, cajoled, and gave me constant encouragement ("How's it coming, Dad?"; "Stick with it"; and words to that effect). My granddaughter, Sophie Cole, twelve, worked wonders with her computer and came up with all sorts of valuable stuff.

Special thanks to my dear friend Barbara Welliver Howe, who accompanied me for interviews and research jaunts and gave me kindly support all along the way. My good pal, confidant, and political guru Tom Houser and onetime able assistant and good friend Sharee Chapman-Schmidt, who provided room and board in Arizona, both weighed in with their backing and ideas.

There's no way I could have completed this book without the timely and invaluable help of Dianne Markus, typist, editor, and organizer extraordinaire.

Rob Taylor, my editor at NTC/Contemporary Publishing Group, somehow kept me more or less on deadline, offered excellent advice and attention along the way, and maintained his "cool" in the face of my sometimes quirky ways. I am grateful also to publisher John Nolan for sensing the worth of this project and forging ahead, to sales director Neal McNish, to project editor Kristen Eberhard, and to Regina Wells, able copyeditor.

The noted Illinois artist-as-reporter Franklin McMahon, my longtime friend, provided a superb graphite drawing of Goldwater with running mate Bill Miller and top campaign aide Dean Burch on the convention floor in San Francisco in 1964. Many of the photos in the book came from the Arizona Historical Foundation's extensive collection in the Hayden Library at Arizona State University in Tempe. My special thanks to Director Evelyn Cooper and her associates, James Allen and Jeff Scott.

The *Arizona Republic* and its staff, especially Charles Kelly, Michael Murphy, Chris Moeser, and Don Harris, did an exceptional job of covering their hometown hero and provided valuable material to me. Two excellent biographies by Lee Edwards and Professor Robert Goldberg were also helpful. My appreciation to Robert Rothenberg, publisher of usa *Today* magazine, and Michelle Stevens of the *Chicago Sun-Times* for publishing several of my articles and columns on Goldwater.

Thanks for everything to Greg and Melissa at the Hermosa Inn in Paradise Valley, and to Jeff, Annette, Jennifer, and Ron Tate at Extended Stay America in Fairfield, down the pike from my hometown of Hamilton, Ohio.

Without such input and assistance from so many, this book might never have come together. My deep appreciation to one and all, and my apologies to any I inadvertently left out.

GOLDWATER

I

Odyssey of an American Original

Excuse me, sir, but didn't you used to be Barry Goldwater?
—ELDERLY WOMAN TO BG

SQUINTING SLIGHTLY, Barry Goldwater peers out at the rust-red and purple mountains beyond the wide windows of his rustic living room. His weathered, carved-in-rock face, geometric jawline, jutting chin, and bony shoulders, a study in sharp angles, seem almost an integral part of the rugged, barren Arizona landscape he loved so passionately.

Barry Goldwater, vanquished presidential contender in 1964 and five-term U.S. senator, invited me to his home midway through his ninth decade of full and exuberant living. As much as any celebrated living

American, he harked back to this nation's simpler yes-
terdays, even before Arizona achieved statehood, yet
evolved into a thoroughly contemporary citizen of
late-twentieth-century America, offering fresh views,
uncomplicated good sense, and uncompromising
integrity. But now he was winding down, feeling the
weight of all those years as a controversial public figure and fierce fighter for freedom. (He died peacefully,
his wife Susan told me, on May 29, 1998, seven months
shy of his ninetieth birthday.)

Staring into the desert valley, past the sturdy,
upright cacti, without shifting his gaze, he told me in
an even tone, "Dick Nixon was a dishonest man who
never told me the truth. Lie after lie. I wouldn't trust
him across that mountain."

I had asked him for his view of United States presidents he had known, and he fairly spit out his recall of
Nixon.

"You endorsed Bob Dole in 1996," I said, "but you
had serious misgivings, didn't you?"

"Frankly, I didn't think he could win. I like him, but
he's got a negative image and kind of a mean streak,
which hurt him. If Colin Powell had entered the race,

I might have backed off Dole. But I told Dole I'd support him, and I keep my word."

How did he feel about Clinton?

"Well, the country won't go to hell under Clinton. I told you awhile back it wasn't going to be easy to defeat him. He's a politician's politician, very articulate with a good brain. He doesn't know much about foreign policy, but he's a quick learner. He's kept the economy on an even keel. I wasn't at all sure he could win in November. I thought he had too much to do to get his ass out of the mud, and I thought we Republicans had a good shot. But he managed all right, and I like Hillary. Did you know she was a 'Goldwater Girl' in '64 back in your state of Illinois? She's got a good head and some gumption."

When I pressed on foreign policy, Goldwater said he sided with Clinton's approach to China.

"In twenty years, if the Chinese get rid of communism—and I think they will—they'll be the leading military power in the world, a great market for U.S. goods."

Goldwater, known as a steadfast hawk on military might, offered what he termed "this sound general rule: Send in U.S. armed forces around the world *only* to defend our freedom. If we go into most of these troubled places with military force, we're going to regret it."

On the scorching summer day (even for the Phoenix area) I last interviewed the senator—with the temperature at 109 degrees Fahrenheit when I pressed the doorbell—I was ushered inside by Luckie Haley, his cheerful Alabama-born housekeeper. "He's waitin' for ya," she told me.

Barry, whom I'd known since several years before his ill-fated presidential campaign, reached forward from deep in his off-white recliner to greet me, his broad, tanned hand gripping mine almost as firmly as three decades earlier.

"Sorry I won't get up, Bill, but my doctor has given me four new hips, two knees, and a shoulder, so I don't get around the way I used to. The doctor's married to my granddaughter, and he's terrific, but I guess it's cost me around a quarter of a million bucks to keep walking. Damn lucky I could afford it."

Perhaps out of deference to his grandson-in-law and his friends on a "couple of hospital boards," he declined my request for a specific opinion on health-care reform, except to say that hospitals and doctors "charge too damn much."

Then he added, "But we need to do something for all the folks who can't afford medical insurance. Many are facing disaster, and I worry about the kids."

Barry was dressed for comfort on this stifling day: his garb could be described as down-home backyard Saturday afternoon in Middle America—T-shirt with broad horizontal red-and-white stripes, beige short shorts, bare feet, and espadrilles parked next to his chair. He was tanned, as always, to the color of a rich wood stain.

Since his crushing defeat by Lyndon Johnson in 1964, in the wake of John F. Kennedy's tragic assassination, Goldwater continued to evolve, taking stands on some hot-button issues that stunned—even infuriated—some of his longtime followers and latter-day conservatives, who, he says, "often don't know what the word [*conservative*] means."

"Of course, I'm still a conservative, always will be," he tells me. "Some folks think I've turned liberal because I believe a woman has a right to an abortion.

That's a decision that's up to the pregnant woman, not up to the pope or some do-gooder or the religious right. It's not a conservative issue at all."

President Reagan's wife, Nancy, in a statement she sent me, notes, "In the 1950s it wasn't fashionable to be conservative, and it took men like Barry and my husband. They found they had a lot in common and made history by igniting the fire of the conservative movement. They believed that the government should simply get out of the way. Barry started a crusade and handed the torch to Ronnie. Everyone's grateful for Barry and what he did for America. He's been a friend from the beginning. . . ."

On issues facing Congress after the Republican sweep in 1994, which ended the long dry spell of the GOP, this was his take on term limits: "Forget it. You are not going to live long enough to see term limits." He wrote off the vaunted Republican "Contract with America"—with a wave of his big hand—as "just another political gimmick."

Before the ethics flap that doomed Newt Gingrich, Goldwater had good things to say about the beleaguered House Speaker. "He's a very knowledgeable, very fine young man whom I once campaigned for, twice in fact, and he lost both elections."

During the late '80s and early '90s, Goldwater had been concerned about what he viewed as extreme intrusions by the religious right into the political process, a violation, he believed, of the constitutional separation of church and state.

"I just hope to God that religious bunch does not grow any stronger, because we're already having enough trouble in our Republican Party without invoking the wrath of God." In a letter he wrote me dated December 30, 1992, he said, "I'm telling you this Republican Party seems like it's hell-bent to destroy itself, and if they keep on going to the right, where the religious groups are, that's exactly what's going to happen."

Despite his macho image as jet pilot and reserve general, and his reputation as a staunch supporter of the Pentagon, Goldwater displayed balance and good sense in his approach to defense policy.

As long ago as 1985, Goldwater and his Democratic counterpart, recently retired Senator Sam Nunn of Georgia, proposed the unthinkable in a 645-page report to Congress: Abolish the Joint Chiefs of Staff, which they described as "an unworkable relic"; rely more on presidential advisers with fewer loyalties to the competing military branches; and stress cooperation rather than narrow catfight competition among the services.

Such reform, which Goldwater termed "my most important initiative in a thirty-year senatorial career," would improve our military capability, he said, while saving billions of tax dollars, which could be employed for underfunded civilian spending on health care, schools, child support and senior programs, drug abuse treatment and prevention, repair of our crumbling infrastructure, and other people programs, possibly even tax relief and certainly progress toward a balanced budget.

Senator Nunn recounted for me this little tale, which gives insight into the Goldwater persona: "Barry and I decided to send a strong letter to the Pentagon about how the service chiefs had overreacted to the preliminary recommendation that their offices be abolished. Naturally, our staff, hoping to avoid a tactical nuclear attack against the Senate Armed Services Committee, drafted a levelheaded, analytical response for our joint signatures.

"Chairman Goldwater reviewed this letter and said, 'Well, this sounds OK, but it just isn't the way I would say it.' The staff responded that they would start over. Barry said, 'Oh, hell no, just throw in a few damns and hells and misspell a few words, and they'll think I wrote it.'"

Goldwater worried about the nagging problems that burden down his beloved country. What can we do, I asked him, to get things straightened out? His answer took me by surprise, even though it was in the Goldwater mold—simple, straightforward, no government involvement:

> Well, I think we've lost the mother complex. A person's mother is the most important factor in any kid's development, whether it's showing kids how to brush their teeth and be clean or teaching them right from wrong.
>
> Mothers aren't around enough these days. They're out working or exercising or going to school or partying or whatever. Most of 'em aren't in close enough contact with their kids. [We need] more mothers being mothers. That's the best way to get kids on the

right track and reduce juvenile delinquency and gangs and violence.

I don't have the answers to crime, but I can tell you more mothers at home is one good answer.

All well and good, of course, but mothers by the millions would tell the senator their families couldn't stay afloat if they didn't work.

Finally, as he glanced at his watch near the end of our long, leisurely visit, I asked him, "What is the most striking change you've observed since you accepted the presidential nomination in San Francisco three decades ago?" He looked again, reflectively, to the mountains in the distance.

"First of all, principle these days has become the lesser of evils. That's not principle. Principle has been almost entirely abandoned in favor of pragmatism. People today don't understand principle, even though this nation was founded on a commitment to bedrock principle.

"Second, the role of money is way out of line. It's strangling us. The influence of money distorts everything in every walk of life. Government of and by the people is waning because of the influence of money in politics. We may already have gone too far to reverse the role and influence of money in our society." Note that this was well before campaign finance reform had become a hot-button issue and a keystone of the presidential campaign of John McCain, Goldwater's successor in the Senate.

As he rose to leave, hoisting himself with still-powerful arms, and walked, stiff-legged and unsteady, like the Tin Woodsman without his oilcan, I was reminded of an encounter he told me about several years after his 1964 presidential campaign: He was on the campaign trail, doing a favor for an old political friend, who was still licking his wounds after narrowly losing a tough primary fight for the Senate seat of the late, legendary Everett McKinley Dirksen, who nominated Goldwater in San Francisco. Barry was sprawled wearily on a stiff, fake leather couch in the Rockford (Illinois) Airport, awaiting the press.

Tired eyes dancing, Barry told me of the "little old lady with blue hair" who approached him timidly on the street.

"Excuse me, sir," she said softly, "but didn't you used to be Barry Goldwater?"

The senator from Arizona smiled. Barry Goldwater, somebody should have told that lady, will always be Barry Goldwater.

There aren't many of his sort left when we need them most. Pity.

2

A Mother's Powerful Influence

My mother was a damn strong woman who'd give me a
good whack when I got out of hand.
—BG TO AUTHOR,
INTERVIEW AT HIS
PARADISE VALLEY HOME,
JULY 1994

BARRY AND HIS SIBLINGS called her "Mun," and she bent the twig early—her way. She became the most important influence in the life of Barry Goldwater, the resolute shaper of America's destiny, values, and reigning philosophy during a span of these past five decades, as his beloved country prepared to embark on the twenty-first century.

Mun was Josephine Williams Goldwater, JoJo to her friends, the tough, slight, unflinching mother of feisty, outspoken, deeply committed Barry and his two younger siblings, Bob and Carolyn.

JoJo Williams, fiercely independent, a deep-dyed patriot from her youth, last-born among six siblings, the only girl on the local baseball team, came by herself to arid Arizona from her modest home in Bowen, Illinois, a dot on the map near Quincy, a Mississippi River town, hoping the bone-dry climate would cure a persistent lung ailment, diagnosed as tuberculosis, a plague at the time.

Barry made no bones about his mother's dominant influence when he and Bob and Carolyn were growing up. She not only ran the household and applied the discipline, but also took the boys on camping trips and engaged in other strenuous outdoor activities. And Barry admitted readily and often that he adored her.

JoJo Williams Goldwater set tough, uncompromising standards. Honesty was paramount, and lying was the unpardonable sin. Her children took her message to heart. Barry never forgave Richard Nixon, once a compatriot, for lying to him about his Watergate involvement, and he even chose not to attend Nixon's funeral.

Soon after she came to Arizona, she met and married Baron Goldwater, said to be a difficult man, detached and aloof, but a merchandising genius who transformed Goldwater's, the ordinary dry goods store he took over from his immigrant forebears in the drab outpost that was then Phoenix, into a highly successful fashion pacesetter, which dealt his family a privileged life.

On his father's side, Barry sprang from a family of intrepid Jewish entrepreneurs from Poland. They were originally named Goldwasser, and Barry's grandfather, Michel Goldwasser, became Michael Goldwater, known as Big Mike, when he came to San Francisco in 1852 from Paris and then London, where he married Sarah Nathan, whose family had a fur-processing factory. Mike had few prospects in Russia-controlled Poland, where Jews were treated as second-class citizens, denied schooling, and limited in their options.

Mike had become a tailor in Paris and later moved to London. When younger brother Joe showed up in London in 1851, Mike heeded the suggestion that opportunities would be far greater in America.

The brothers were doers. In their first stab at business, they opened a saloon below a second-floor bordello in Sonora, California, a mining town about 100 miles east of San Francisco. In due course, the saloon failed, as did a second saloon and store that Joe opened. This was to be a common occurrence in their early years in the United States, but they were undaunted. After a fling in Los Angeles, they made their first foray into still-primitive Arizona. With Joe's backing, Mike bought a wagon and four mules and hauled merchandise into Gila City, a gold-mining camp east of what is now Yuma. That operation also went broke, but the Goldwater brothers' optimism seemed unlimited, and they stayed the course.

It was a hazardous undertaking. En route back from Prescott, Arizona, in 1872, where they bid on army contracts, they were attacked by thirty or so Yavapai Indians. Joe was shot in the back and shoulder, and bullets penetrated Mike's hat and a partner's shirt. All three might have been killed if three ranchers hadn't shown up to drive off the Indians.

In 1883, Joe's store in Bisbee was the focal point of the Bisbee Massacre. Gunmen who held up the store panicked and fatally shot four bystanders on the street outside. Joe eventually was forced to empty the safe and survived the robbery to testify against the robbers, all of whom were hanged.

None of the dangers and financial difficulties could keep the Goldwaters down. Morris Goldwater, son of Mike, and Barry's role model and mentor, opened a general store in the new village of Phoenix in 1872. It closed three years later, and the Goldwaters concentrated on a successful store in Prescott.

Morris turned out to be one of the leading figures in the early history of Arizona. He was a founder of the dominant Arizona Democratic Party, and even though Barry, his nephew, ended up a lifelong Republican, Morris took the young man under his wing, especially after Barry's father died when Barry was a freshman at the University of Arizona.

Off and on, Morris served seven terms as mayor of Prescott over nearly half a century and also held territorial and state posts, including president of the Council in the twentieth Territorial Legislature, vice president of the Arizona Constitutional Convention, which paved the way for statehood in 1912, when Barry was three, and president of the Senate for the second Arizona State Legislature in 1914.

The resilient Goldwaters, who tried and failed at many business enterprises, finally clicked famously in retailing. In 1896, the family got back into business in Phoenix, building a dry goods store at 18–20 North First Avenue. Barry's father, Baron, was general manager and something of a visionary in building Goldwater's as a retail fashion hub for the Southwest and providing wealth to his family.

Barry was fond of recounting the story of how his ingenious forebears "raised the seed money" to launch their successful retail venture. "It was all quite illegal," Barry said impishly. "They had this hauling operation, and they appropriated—you might say hijacked—this load of Levi Strauss dungarees, jeans today, in California. They crossed the line into Arizona and set up shop. That's a helluva lot easier than getting a loan without collateral from some bank."

Mimicking the familiar campaign pitch of political strivers intent on emulating Abe Lincoln, Barry once joked, "I was born in a log cabin," then added with a chuckle, "with a swimming pool and tennis court."

Baron Goldwater, by Barry's account, was a distant father. Barry didn't doubt his father's love but didn't feel he was "much of a father." By most accounts, Baron was dapper, formal, fashionable, self-absorbed, and somewhat disengaged from the real world.

"Dad couldn't even drive a car," Bob Goldwater told me.

It was, of course, an era when most mothers stayed home and cared for the house and children, while fathers were the somewhat remote breadwinners and occasional parents. There were no Oprahs around to impart "touchy-feely" wisdom and inspire family closeness, and there were precious few popular books to guide parents every step of the way.

Barry Jr., now sixty-two, living for the past few years in a guest house at the Goldwaters' Scorpion Hill home, felt a similar distance from his father.

"We knew he loved us," the younger Goldwater told me recently, "but he didn't show it. We had kind of an arm's-length relationship. Even during the fourteen years I was in Congress, we had very little contact. Every so often, we'd have a hamburger in his Senate office, but I can recall only two times when he dropped by my office. And we almost never talked politics or discussed issues. He didn't give out much advice, except to say I should be my own man and be honest."

When he was a small boy, Barry Jr. recalls, even before the all-encompassing demands of his father's political life, "Dad wasn't around much, and he always seemed preoccupied." During World War II, while Barry did not see combat, he ferried cargo planes endlessly across the Atlantic and was away for long stretches.

Baron and JoJo's first child, Barry Morris Goldwater, developed his tough hide and exuberant, impulsive, often rebellious spirit in his hardscrabble birthplace, where the earth was barren and scraped raw, where sturdy cacti punctuated the harsh setting and the temperature rises above 110 degrees Fahrenheit, where survival was both a worry and a challenge.

Barry Goldwater, unpredictable godfather of conservatism's rise as a powerful force in America, will leave an indelible imprint on the political landscape. The quintessential frontiersman, he was born on January 1, 1909, in the tiny, primitive village of Phoenix nearly three years before Arizona was admitted as the forty-eighth state. A craggy, bronzed prototype of the rugged, self-reliant, free-thinking westerner, Goldwater thus lived all but one decade of the momentous twentieth century.

From early on, young Barry was a handful. Mischievous, earthy, devil-may-care, all boy, as the saying goes. His mother kept him more or less in check, but his no-nonsense, barely involved father refused to tolerate Barry's antics and marginal schoolwork. ("Hell, I got kicked out of school," Barry said later.) So Baron Goldwater packed off his elder son to a military setting in Virginia where the "young renegade" might acquire both discipline and polish far from home. Together, father and son made the long, dreary, cross-country train trip to Staunton Military Academy. Barry remembered that his father barely uttered a word on their journey and dropped him off with a $5 bill two miles from the school. "Find your way," he ordered.

Barry got off to a rocky start at Staunton. He resented school regulations that required first-year students to act as virtual "valets" to upper classmen, and he got his first taste of prejudice when some classmates called him "Goldberg" because of his Jewish antecedents. This cut deep and made a lasting impression on Barry, who vowed never to engage in such cruelty. Yet, in his presidential bid, he was unfairly accused of racism, one of many slanderous and untrue charges hurled against him. In due course, his grades improved somewhat, and as a junior, he encountered Major

Alexander (Sandy) Patch, a faculty member who became a lifelong role model for young Barry. Under Major Patch's patient guidance, Barry found himself. He became a first-rate athlete—he was captain of the swim team and played varsity football, basketball, and track, where he threw the javelin. He was elected class treasurer and captain of "C" Company, as well as chair of the student honor committee and custodian of the academy's ideals of "truth, honor, and duty"—a motto that made a lasting impression and helped mold the man he would become.

Barry returned home at age eighteen, having tasted honors and acclaim in prep school, and enrolled at the state university in Tucson, known as a "party" school. He focused on cars, girls, and clothes and paid little heed to academics. Barry admittedly was never a scholar and once said he didn't have "a first-class brain," even though his solid judgment and keen instincts more than made up for the absence of formal academic training. At one point, as Barry embarked on his political career, his mother chided him: "I'm surprised the smart one didn't run," referring to brother Bob, a Stanford graduate.

After his lackluster freshman year, he withdrew from the University of Arizona following the death of his father at age sixty-two in 1929; Bob said that gave Barry an excuse to leave school and go to work at the Goldwater store, where he concentrated on the merchandising side. Brother Bob came to work seven years later and assumed the burdens of the business office. They became an effective tandem in building the retail operation and the reputation of Goldwater's as the dominant fashion hub of the Southwest.

But Barry was restless and too multifaceted in his interests to remain forever in the world of commerce. It was inevitable he would gravitate to the wider world.

"Money and math are not my thing," he once told me. "I like to have money and spend money—but I don't like to worry about it."

As he ceded more of the burdens to Bob, Barry became something of a whirling dervish in the civic arena, actively joining such fraternal groups as the Elks, Shriners, and Masons, all the while tilting toward the political realm without fully realizing or acknowledging that bent. He became president of the Phoenix

Chamber of Commerce and got deeply involved in city affairs.

"Phoenix had lousy city government back then," Bob Goldwater told me, "and Barry and I and Harry Rosenzweig—a close lifelong friend—were determined to do something about it. A movement got under way to replace what we considered an incompetent city council. At a meeting to select reform-minded candidates, Harry said they ended up short two guys—and he told 'em he and Barry would run. They did, and Barry led the ticket."

During this period, he pursued his twin passions of photography and flying. Flight became almost a religious experience for Goldwater, who was not drawn to organized religion, and he became an accomplished jet pilot, flying more than 150 types of aircraft in his lifetime, and rising to the rank of reserve general. His photos of the singular, often starkly dramatic Arizona landscape and the distinctive faces of Arizona's Native Americans won wide acclaim and earned him election to the Royal Photographic Society of London while he was still in his twenties.

But most serious on Barry's agenda, and uppermost in his mind, was Margaret (Peggy) Johnson, stylish daughter of wealthy Borg-Warner executive Ray Prescott Johnson from Muncie, Indiana. He had met Peggy when she and her mother came shopping at the Goldwaters' Phoenix store in December 1930. According to Barry, the Johnsons came to Arizona hoping the mild, dry climate would help Peggy's brother cure a persistent bronchial condition.

"I remember thinking she was a rather pretty girl," he said, "with very deep blue eyes and a beautiful complexion. She told me later she was depressed at the thought of missing all the good Christmas parties in Muncie. She thought Phoenix was a hick town, and I didn't make much of an impression on her. She said she was going to Mount Vernon Seminary in Washington, D.C. I told her I had graduated from Staunton in Virginia."

Herb Green, a friend, brought Peggy to the Goldwater home on Central Avenue for a party that Christmas season, "but it was a big affair, and I didn't pay any particular attention to Herb's date."

Soon thereafter, by Barry's admission, he was struck: "The next time I saw her, in 1932, the little girl from Mount Vernon Seminary had become a ravishingly beautiful, mature woman. She had come back to

Phoenix to be with her father, who was desperately ill. I tried to see her as often as possible, but she had other things on her mind.

"When her father died, Peggy and her mother returned to Muncie, and I became something of a commuter. She was fun to be with. I liked her sense of humor, her independence, her throaty laugh, her eyes.

"I was in love."

Barry soon showed in matters of the heart the same impulsive ways that marked his political career. "I first proposed after a two-week visit in the summer of 1933. Peggy said she wasn't ready to get married. She wasn't sure about Arizona, and she wasn't sure about me. But I was sure, and I told her so.

"I went to Muncie the day after Christmas, by which time things had simmered down at the store, to spend the rest of the holidays. New Year's Eve, Peggy and I were at a dance. She wanted to call and wish her mother a Happy New Year. When we were in the telephone booth, I told her I was running out of money and out of patience. For the umpteenth time, I asked her to marry me. She said yes."

In January 1934, before they were married, Peggy had been expected to accompany her mother on a long-planned world cruise. Barry was tormented by the thought of the long separation and the worry she might encounter someone else on shipboard or ashore.

Leaving nothing to chance, "I made sure there was a packet of letters waiting for her whenever the cruise ship docked." She kept them until her death in 1985 after their fifty-first anniversary.

Through all the moments of triumph in Barry's life, as well as the sorrow, Barry said Peggy has been "my strength, my companion, a part of my private world where no other human beings, not even our children, have been allowed to enter."

This shows the warmer side of a political figure whom much of the outside world has seen as crusty, obdurate, tough, even somewhat remote.

They were married nine months after his phone-booth proposal in an Episcopal service in Muncie, despite family pause because of Barry's Jewish heritage. Peggy, smitten at first by his bold ways and good looks, became Barry's faithful and totally committed partner in whatever he chose to do, even though neither politics nor flying nor the outdoor life was her cup of tea.

Their four children, Joanne, Barry Jr. (who served seven terms in Congress from California and then lost a race for the U.S. Senate), Michael, and Peggy Jr., felt, in varying degrees, some of the same isolation from their father that Barry had experienced in his youth. Barry and Peggy were said to be deeply in love, but they drifted apart in later years, the result of their long separations and her growing dislike of politics. When Peggy died in December 1985 of emphysema and heart failure, after fifty-one years of marriage, Barry was devastated and left feeling desolate and depressed.

3

A Renaissance Man's Dream House and Diversions

I'm going to stay the way I've been all my life.
Even though I haven't got a hell of a lot of years left,
I'm going to have fun living them.
—BG, LETTER TO AUTHOR,
JULY 12, 1994

EVEN AS A BOY OF TWELVE, Barry Goldwater looked ahead. He had ideas. He knew what he wanted.

With brother Bob and several friends, he camped overnight on Scorpion Hill, at the edge of what Barry later called "that dusty little frontier town" of Phoenix, overlooking the capacious valley and surrounded by the bare, rough-cut mountains in the distance.

Young Barry lay in his bedroll and peered up at a million stars that pierced the black sky and the moon that seemed almost near enough to touch. To Barry, this was as close to heaven as a boy could get.

He had a plan.

"When I grow up, I want to live up here," he said.

And he never forgot. Thirty-six years later, in 1957–58, he built the rambling, rustic house of his dreams on Scorpion Hill, the home he loved, where he lived the last four decades of his life, and where he died just shy of ninety with his family and memories around him.

"A fellow named Brophy," Barry told me, "sold me forty acres up here, including the homesite, for $25,000 and thought he made a killing." An acre in those choice environs today is worth many times the total price he paid for forty acres then, and Goldwater sold off some acreage over the years to meet expenses that soared beyond the modest Senate salary of those days. After his death, the children began exploring sale of the house he called "Be-Nun-I-Kin," Navajo for "house on top of the hill," a kind of tribute to his many Native American friends. By April of 2000, it had been placed on the market. "I've probably spent more time with Arizona's Indians than any other white man," he said.

Navajos also gave Barry a tribal name, "Chischilly," for the "curly haired one."

That Paradise Valley home atop Scorpion Hill is vintage Goldwater, classic Southwest. It is a mass of sharp angles, like Goldwater himself, with his spare, chiseled features and lean lines. Its material and colors somehow fit the man: stone and slate, earth tones and weathered woods. So do its artifacts and plantings: prickly cactus, paintings of the Old West, sculptures of fierce and friendly Indians, the lonely range rider, countless family and political photos, books, plaques, and awards everywhere, and Barry himself in various guises as pilot, intrepid cowboy, outdoorsman, husband, father, senator.

His desk is huge, geometric and built-in, looking out on two sides at breathtaking views of the now teeming valley and unchanging mountains. Near at hand is a mass of electronic gear to put him in touch with the wider world. The desk is mainly clean, as he left it, free of papers, except for a typed schedule and sophisticated Nikon 35 mm camera, what he used to shoot his legendary photos of the trademark flora and fauna of his beloved Arizona, and his friends and favorite subjects, the Native Americans from twenty Arizona tribes, whose parchment faces and severe looks matched the landscape.

Down a long hall off the living room is a handsome, lifelike portrait of Barry, circa 1963 or 1964, by Norman Rockwell, the celebrated painter of American nostalgia and magazine covers that captured simpler times.

There is a dramatic three-foot-high sculpture of Barry brandishing a rifle on a galloping horse. There are oil portraits of Barry in aviator gear and standing tall in open-shirt western regalia. There is a heroic bronze bust. There are literally hundreds of family and political photos scattered throughout the house. The powder room is papered wall-to-wall, even its ceiling, with black-and-white photos.

In his cluttered workshop is a long, built-in bench strewn with tools and plane parts; sleek model planes line the walls and hang from the ceiling. When I saw it again after his death, it appeared untouched. Barry's love affair with airplanes was unending.

A room farther down the hall housed his massive gun collection, handguns and long guns, some highly ornate and with historical significance.

At twelve, Barry was both different and special. He was not very good in school, a poor reader, often distracted, and possibly afflicted with what wife Susan believes would have been diagnosed today as dyslexia. But his native brilliance came out in other ways. It was a time before the electronic marvels that we take for granted, even as they multiply before we can grasp and understand them. Even radio was in its infancy, and Barry was a born tinkerer. When he was eleven, his father bought him a crystal radio receiver. There were no radio stations in Phoenix then, so "I spent hours picking up music and news from as far away as Los Angeles." Barry became a ham operator, tapping out messages in Morse code on a simple ten-watt sending unit. He pursued his interest, and in the early 1920s, at the age of twelve, he helped Earl Neilson, a radio shop owner, set up KFAD, the first primitive commercial radio station in Phoenix. This was among the many diversions he mastered and loved. "Radios and gadgets have been part of my life ever since," Goldwater said. He stayed with his hobby all his life and became expert in communicating around the globe. Even Walter Cronkite knew of his prowess, telling me, "As a sidelight of his personal pursuit of his patriotic service, he [Goldwater] spent hundreds of hours at his beloved amateur shortwave radio station in his Arizona home providing a telephone line between GIs in Vietnam and their parents in the United States."

Phoenix today is a surging metropolis of 2.9 million, the nation's sixth largest city, and continuing its spectacular growth. But when Barry was a boy, it was a dusty cow town of maybe ten thousand. To earn a little extra spending money, he picked cotton—long staple cotton, for the finest shirts and other garments—in what was to become downtown Phoenix. There is a splendid irony here, for Barry in the 1960s was unfairly and wrongly accused of racism, and it was poor blacks who were relegated to most of the nation's cotton picking.

Most of Barry's time in the final years was spent inside the home that was so much a part of him. In the ninth decade of his incredible, eventful life, his rustic castle became his refuge from the world outside.

In February 1992, he married Susan Wechsler, who is, as Barry's mother was, a nurse. She runs Hospice of the Valley, the largest hospice in Arizona, with 600 employees, 500 volunteers, and a $33 million annual budget. A charming, upbeat, take-charge woman, she gave him new uplift in his life, friends say, and encouraged him to continue expressing his controversial views, thought by some to veer off from his more rigid conservatism of yore. Susan is often credited—or blamed—for his increasingly open-minded approach to "hot-button" issues, such as his stances accepting abortion and gays in the military, but she maintains flatly that nobody's influence, including hers, could change her husband's mind on matters that mattered to him, and he stated repeatedly that these stances were outside his definition of conservative.

In September 1996, he had the first of several small frontal lobe strokes, which affected his memory and his pinpoint insights into his political past.

But Susan says "he remained strong physically, with all his organs in good shape," and enjoyed the steady stream of visitors, including longtime friends, and even Bill and Hillary Clinton on separate occasions. He was active around the house, she said, "but I never could get him to pick up his socks," a common plaint of the world's wives.

He was "needy" and often depressed. "From time to time," she told me, "I had to give him hell to get him going."

What is so remarkable about Barry Goldwater is the astounding diversity of his interests. Here was a man with thirty years in the U.S. Senate and an exhausting, frustrating presidential run, who also engaged in a variety of unrelated activities, each of which could have been a "career" for many men. In these, he didn't merely dabble; he mastered them and became expert in pursuing them.

Everywhere in his home was evidence of a life filled to overflowing beyond the demanding realm of politics, testimony to his qualities as a true Renaissance man. One wonders how he could possibly cram so much into his years. Said Bob, "Barry loved his hobbies. He was good at them, and they gave him great joy."

His myriad interests included photography, flying, hunting, and gun collecting.

His brilliance as a photographer was recognized early. As a young man in his twenties, he was invited to join the Royal Photographic Society of London, an honor usually reserved for those whose lifework was exceptional photography. His friendship with Ansel Adams, often described as the dean of American photographers, extended over a half century. His photographs are collected at the Arizona Historical Foundation on the Arizona State University campus and are displayed widely in private collections and museums.

This is Barry's own account of his "career" as a master photographer:

> Photography was one of my later hobbies. My wife gave me a little reflex camera as a present. We had a small apartment then. It was necessary to use the kitchen as a darkroom. Peggy didn't like that because it smelled up the place.
>
> A chance conversation got me into photography in a big way. Since I'd collected many books and historical records on Arizona, the Southwest, and Mexico, students at Arizona State University would stop by the house and use them for reference. One day a young fellow asked me if I'd ever seen a photo of Pipe Springs, Arizona. I'd been there, but I didn't have a picture of it. The chat made a big impression on me. It showed a need for local photographs. Obviously, there had to be many other Pipe Springs.

From then on, I carried a camera on every trip to take photos for the historical record. Later I bought a movie camera and filmed a rafting trip down the Colorado River in the summer of 1940. The 700-mile journey combined three hobbies—photography, rafting, and hiking.

I embarked on the six-week trip with five other men and three women in three boats. It was an exhausting forty-two days, filled with rapids, sharp winds, bug bites, and enough sand in different parts of my body to build a sizable kid's castle on any beach. Part of my diary on those days reads:

"Sleeping in the open under God's own sky is one of the most overrated of all acts of man or woman. Forty-two nights of huffing and puffing my lungs into the deep recesses of a rubber void, known as an air mattress, have convinced me that an innerspring has 10,000 advantages.

"Bugs of all sizes have promenaded over my body from top to bottom. Bugs with only a cursory interest have wandered over me and with no more than a 'humph,' have let me be. Others, carrying knives, sabers, and broken bottles, have passed my way and left a diverse collection of tools of torture firmly implanted in my being. As a result of their nocturnal visits, I have as fine a collection of bumps and itches as any man ever supported. The lovely thing about these bites is they never itch until one is almost asleep."

I started showing film of that trip up and down the state, narrating it more than a hundred times. Those visits were a big help when I started out in politics. When Howard Pyle ran for governor in 1950 [Goldwater helped run his campaign], I knew people in almost every town we visited.

I developed my own film. At one time, I had more than 15,000 negatives and some twenty-five miles of film. Much of that has already gone to Arizona State University. Some 8,000 negatives remain to be identified.

Photography began paying off around the country, too. Various galleries offered photo exhibits of my Indian work as well as Grand Canyon and desert scenes. More than 250 showings, including a good number in Europe, took the state of Arizona far beyond its boundaries. I eventually became an associate member of the Royal Photographic Society of London and had several books of photographs published. My scrapbooks show shots from Phoenix to Paris to Pakistan.

Many rank as photographic classics. Barry was to photography what Georgia O'Keeffe was to painting.

Barry was also a "phenomenal pilot," says brother Bob. In his lifetime, he logged more than 12,000 hours in 165 kinds of aircraft, ranging from early biplanes with open cockpits to late-model private and military jets, and including helicopters and gliders. He was the first nonrated test pilot to fly the celebrated U-2, and he flew the B-1 bomber, F-104, French Mirage, and German-French A-300. He flew the SR-71 at a speed of Mach 3 at an altitude of 83,000 feet. He was addicted all his life to aviation.

In his autobiographies, Barry tells how in 1929, at age twenty, he "took up flying," adding, "Bob was what you might call my first victim":

> I began slipping out the back door of the house about dawn. My mother later told me she had thought it was a sunrise romance with one of the town's fair maidens. Indeed, I'd found true love—the airplane.
>
> Bob mentioned Mother's guess to me. It was time to confess. I said he could come with me some morning. Bob happily agreed. We had to make one stop first, at the small flying field southeast of town (now Sky Harbor International Airport, with a main terminal named for one Barry M. Goldwater) to look at a plane.

When we arrived, I coaxed him into the passenger's seat and climbed into the cockpit. He hollered, "What the hell's going on?"

I took off and flew around Phoenix, and he has never completely trusted me since. My mother, finding out what happened, later said over breakfast, "Barry, why didn't you tell me you were taking flying lessons. I would have gone, too." She meant it.

"Most small boys dream about flying," Barry said. "Our gang watched the crop dusters and barnstormers around Phoenix. . . . I soloed in 1929. One of my first passengers was a girlfriend of my pal Harry Rosenzweig. We were doing a tight 360 degrees at about 2,000 feet over her house, when, bingo, the plane snapped over and went into a spin. Those early instructors rarely taught students how to get out of a spin. One of them once said jokingly to me, 'If you ever get into one, let go of everything and start the Lord's Prayer.' That sure as hell wasn't going to solve my problem, so I grabbed the damn stick with both hands and instead took a deep breath to ease the tension. The trainer finally leveled out, and we landed. I took Joanne home and downed two shots of straight bourbon to stop my hands from shaking. I was back flying the next day—solo.

"My dream of becoming an Army Air Corps pilot lingered. The corps had rejected me as an aviation cadet because of poor vision. But I never gave up the hope of wearing its wings. The store work meant only eating—flying with the corps would be living. . . . I did a lot of flying up in Navajo country. The tribe had some wicked winters; I'd collect food and hay and drop them to the Indian families and cattle cut off by snowdrifts."

"A major part of my life," flying for Barry had been almost a religious experience. "Perhaps it is the splendid isolation of being alone in the air which fascinates me," he said, "or it might be the perspective which comes from looking down on every part of the world—rivers and oceans and cities and hamlets. I see the lights, and I wonder where they are burning—in a young couple's home where they have just put the babies to bed, in a widow's lonely house, or perhaps in a store like Goldwater's when I was a boy. . . . Any pilot can describe the mechanics of flying. What it can do for the spirit of man is beyond description. When you are flying at night in a modern jet at 30,000 feet, the skies and stars are infinite. The entire universe seems to be saying, 'Oh, God, how great thou art.' The heavens endure; men come and go.

"Some pilots claim flying gives them a sense of power or mastery over objects on the ground. My feelings in the air take me in an opposite direction. When man conquered the sky, he didn't create anything. All he did was take advantage of the laws of physics. Our piston engines are an example of this, and our jet engines are an extension of that example, and all of it is made possible by Him who created this orderly, always consistent universe."

This is Barry Goldwater expressing his thoughts and feelings more than two decades ago. Never a regular churchgoer, he was a man of great faith and believer in a divine being:

"My faith in the future rests squarely on the belief that man, if he doesn't first destroy himself, will find new answers in the universe, new technologies, new disciplines, which will contribute to a vastly different and better world in the twenty-first century. Recalling what has happened in my short lifetime in the fields of communication and transportation and the life sciences, I marvel at the shortsighted pessimists who tell us we have reached our productive capacity, who project a future consisting primarily of dividing what we now have and making do with less. To my mind, the single essential element on which all new discoveries are dependent is *human freedom*.

"All history is the record of man's quest for freedom. At the moment, to fly an airplane is the ultimate extension of individual freedom. We have penetrated outer space. We have sent men to the moon and brought them home. But in this limitless world of the sky, nature's immutable laws must be obeyed. And man is still subservient to the dictates of his Creator."

In what Barry Goldwater says about flight, there is some of the poet, some of the dreamer, some of the visionary, facets of his character largely undiscovered during his long political career, especially during his '64 campaign for president, when he was painted as somewhat simplistic, unlettered, banal, and worse.

On one visit to his Senate office in 1983, I admired the dramatic plane photos on every wall and asked if he was flying much lately. He was seventy-four and had endured heart bypass surgery and hip and knee replacements. He looked as well as ever, strong and tanned.

"I've got fifty-five years in as a pilot," he said. "I can still fly, but only solo in helicopters these days or with another pilot. I won't run the risk of taking somebody down with me."

Well into his eighties, he continued to build beautiful and authentic model planes in his home workshop. When I visited his home in early 2000, the bench top was strewn with tools and parts, apparently just as he left it.

Other hobbies of Barry's were hunting and gun collecting. An avid lover of the outdoors, he hunted whenever he could break away and rode the rapids on the Colorado River. Bob remembers when he and Barry, who did everything together, on their once-a-year hunt for deer, met Clark Gable on the rim of the Grand Canyon. They hunted ducks and doves, too, and went after buffalo on the plains between Prescott and Flagstaff.

In his home, a room is devoted to a vast gun collection of every age, style, and variety, including some he finished and decorated himself, all manner of guns, old and new, long guns and handguns, mounted on the wall and in glass cases. Many revert back to those used on the range and in old cowboy and Indian movies.

When I questioned him about the proliferation of guns in our society, and the increasing numbers of gun deaths, even in schools, he said emphatically, "Effective, across-the-board gun control is impossible."

"But don't the 200 million guns in private hands contribute to the upsurge in crime?" I asked.

"Probably so," he responded, "but the number is probably closer to 400 million, and there's nothing we can do, even if it makes sense."

Goldwater was a contemporary of the late beloved actor Jimmy Stewart, remembered fondly for his role in *It's a Wonderful Life*, the nostalgic Christmas-season classic. In the late summer of 1994, Barry gave testimony in a letter to me to his own wonderful life. "Bill, I'm going to stay the way I've been all my life. Even though I haven't got a hell of a lot of years left, I'm going to have fun living them."

That is exactly what he did until the end, says Susan Goldwater.

4

What *Conservatism* Meant to Its Godfather

A lot of so-called conservatives today don't know what the word means.
—BG TO AUTHOR,
INTERVIEW AT HIS PARADISE
VALLEY HOME, JULY 1994

BARRY GOLDWATER set down his guidelines for pure, traditional conservatism in *Conscience of a Conservative*, a little book published in 1960 that inspired millions of Americans, many young and questing. This was a joint effort with Brent Bozell, devoted conservative, eloquent writer, and brother-in-law of William F. Buckley. The first printing was a modest 10,000, but eventually the book sold an astounding 3.5 million copies, an unqualified bestseller, and became the bible of the conservative movement.

Goldwater's definition of his conservative philosophy, as he stated it carefully to me in his living room, is "very simple":

"A conservative is a person who wants to apply the proven values of the past to the problems and challenges of today. It's a dynamic, living philosophy, just as our Constitution is a living document subject to new interpretations in view of changing circumstances." It is from this seemingly bland blueprint that angry disagreement erupted.

"One problem today," Goldwater told me with obvious feeling, "is with these neoconservatives, the radical right, the religious extremists whose interpretation is very narrow and who want to destroy everybody who doesn't agree with 'em. I see them as betrayers of the fundamental principles of conservatism. A lot of so-called conservatives today don't know what the word means."

Goldwater reacted predictably when antiabortion rightist Rev. Jerry Falwell condemned President Reagan's nomination of Sandra Day O'Connor to the Supreme Court:

"I'm getting a little tired of people in this country raising hell because they don't happen to subscribe to the position a person has. A president could offer the Lord's name and you would find some of these outfits opposed. I am probably one of the most conservative members of Congress, and I don't like to get kicked around by people who call themselves conservative on a nonconservative matter," he grumbled.

"If it's going to be a fight in the Senate, you are going to find Old Goldy fighting like hell."

That tirade tells a lot about the craggy, cantankerous Arizonan.

As the godfather of twentieth-century conservatism, Goldwater preached the canons, paved the way, took the blows for the ascent of Ronald Reagan. In the presidential campaign of 1964, Reagan, then a TV pitchman for General Electric, got national exposure by articulating the conservative credo on national TV for Republican nominee Goldwater. Ever the polished communicator, Reagan made an impact that upstaged Goldwater and left the former actor as heir apparent.

Goldwater concluded that various groups in the United States donned the mantle of increasingly popular conservatism to push their own agendas dominated by narrow views on abortion and homosexuality. Neither, he says, is a conservative or liberal issue.

Goldwater took intense heat and gratuitous carping for his stands favoring pro-choice and gays in the military from longtime backers and "neoconservatives" who wrongly felt he was gradually abandoning his staunch conservatism.

He vehemently denied the charge, stressing repeatedly that abortion and homosexuality were not part of the classic conservative doctrine and did not even remotely equate with such noble conservative fundamentals as "life, liberty, and the pursuit of happiness." In many respects, Goldwater took the libertarian view that government should have at most a minimal role in the lives of private citizens.

"Freedom," Goldwater always said, "is the single word that has expressed my political philosophy all during my public life."

There is, however, a stance he came to embrace in the mid-'90s that until now has not been known to more than a relative few, and that would have touched off a raging national firestorm had it been widely revealed while he was alive: Barry Goldwater favored the legalization of drugs.

This stunning revelation came after discussions over several years with his "dear friend" publisher Bill

Buckley, who long had urged decriminalization of drugs; his brother Bob, who agreed; and wife Susan, his latter-day confidant and sounding board. It was not in any sense a repudiation of his conservatism; it was rather an assertion of his libertarian belief that drug use by an individual is the private right of a free human being. Susan Goldwater told me recently that her husband came to believe passionately in what some would see as an incongruous position. But he stoutly maintained that it was consistent with his long-held philosophy that made preeminent the rights of the individual.

There were also practical aspects to Goldwater's decision.

He likened the situation to the widespread consumption of alcohol in society today and the unconditional final failure of prohibition in 1933. Legalizing drugs, he said, would end the sham of vast illegal profits by drug importers, dealers, and distributors, and the bribing of police and others in and outside law enforcement to permit the flow of forbidden substances.

The chief argument against legalization is the claim that drug use and addiction would surge. But there is no solid research to confirm that the easy availability of drugs would greatly spur their popularity and usage over the long haul, and Goldwater dismissed this argument. He became convinced that legalization on balance would have a positive impact and viewed as a major plus the potential of taxing legal drugs to provide funds—sadly lacking today—for prevention and treatment.

Of the more than two million Americans in U.S. prisons at the dawn of this new century—far more than anywhere else in the world—at least half, and possibly as many as 65 percent, are incarcerated for low-level drug offenses. Many of these are about the age of Barry's grandchildren and are young, nonviolent first offenders, caught in some campus or community with a small bag of marijuana for their personal use, convicted, and sent to prison for five and more years under punitive determinate-sentencing laws.

The incredible cost of this wrongheaded imprisonment amounts to billions of tax dollars, which enrich the "prison-industrial complex" (apologies to President Eisenhower, who coined the phrase "military-industrial complex" to identify the defense contractors who profit and lobby for new, often unneeded, weapons and systems and contribute to a bloated military budget). This sucks away funds desperately needed for education, child and elder care, health protection, repair of crumbling infrastructure, and other urgent people needs.

Knowing the uproar that any public declaration would cause, Goldwater quietly pursued the issue of drug legalization in his later years with a small circle of friends and family whom he trusted.

His position on drugs—probably contrary to the views of at least two-thirds of his most avid supporters—demonstrates anew the integrity of the man and his willingness to embrace the unpopular, to challenge the conventional wisdom, to follow the dictates of his judgment and his readings of what would serve his nation best.

A *Washington Post* interview on July 28, 1994, with reporter Lloyd Grove was headlined "Barry Goldwater's Left Turn." Goldwater responded testily, "There was no left turn. I'm still the conservative I've always been and always will be."

When Grove needled Goldwater about "an unlikely new career as a gay rights activist," Goldwater shot back, "The big thing is to make this country, along with every other country in the world with a few exceptions, quit discriminating against people just because they're gay. You don't have to agree with it, but they have a constitutional right to be gay. And that's what brings me into it."

Goldwater told me his support for gays in the military was "no big deal," explaining, "I'm sure there were gays in Hannibal's army, but they didn't have a prying press to write about it."

The *Post* interview continued, "Having spent thirty-seven years of my life in the military as a reservist, and never having met a gay in all that time, and never having even talked about it in all those years, I just thought why the hell shouldn't they serve? They're American citizens. As long as they're not doing things that are harmful to anybody else. . . ."

Goldwater has a grandson who's gay, and his brother has a gay granddaughter. "We're sort of at a loss to know what the hell it's all about," he admitted, but he said emphatically that their status didn't influence his stand.

In 1992, he infuriated local party wheelhorses by backing Karan English, a Democrat, for Congress; she won over a Christian conservative Republican. Barry was unmoved by the tempest he created with his departure from party regularity.

"Hell, the Republican fellow came here from Washington because he thought he could practically steal the seat. Hadn't been here long enough to spell Arizona before he announced. And he told everybody he was my good buddy, which he wasn't. That gal was the best choice," he said.

"When she got elected, my Republican friends were all set to scalp me. They wanted to take my name off the Republican headquarters, the airport, and the high school. Intolerant as hell. But it all blew over, and nothing happened."

The metamorphosis of the past twenty years involved no radical shift, but was more a mellowing, a sorting out of what fit Goldwater's parameters of his "true" conservatism and what didn't. He was still a partisan Republican but was comfortable straying from the party line when he felt the urge.

The key to understanding the stubborn uniqueness of Barry Goldwater is to grasp the underlying premise of "his" conservatism. It came down to individual liberty, which to him was the inalienable birthright of every American.

In truth, Goldwater, despite a variety of questions and challenges, was damnably consistent. The confusion arises from the inaccurately breathless discovery by press and public, including many avid supporters, that he turned liberal in the last two decades of his life; they cited his stands on abortion rights and gays in the military and throughout society. These positions, which he enunciated after his Senate service ended, set teeth gnashing among the religious right and other hard-line segments of society.

They missed the point. There was no sharp "left turn" in Goldwater's philosophy, as the *Washington Post* wrongly characterized it. Rather, there was an evolutional recognition that these positions fit his long-held "libertarian" criteria.

These were not, he said over and over, elements of "conservative" dogma, but rather controversial examples of the right of free citizens to exercise their freedom, to do as they choose within the bounds of law, a posture he always embraced.

"A lot of folks simply don't understand, and the media always either oversimplify or complicate everything," he told me. "People seek to justify and validate their biases under the conservative banner, which has become increasingly popular and even dominant. But they really aren't conservative—or even liberal—issues. I've said it often: a lot of people who claim to be 'conservative' don't understand the meaning of the word."

Goldwater was not a deep thinker on crime, and he was not a lawyer, but he came out on the common-sense side of the issue rather than the often mindless, safe, "tough-on-crime" stance that hasn't worked, often is counterproductive, and has led to a prison-building binge that sucks away billions of tax dollars from programs that benefit ordinary people. The "tough on crime" battle cry is also a catchphrase of what Goldwater called the neo- or pseudoconservatives, but it isn't, he argued, a legitimate facet of true conservatism.

On youth crime, he told me, "Part of the answer is more mothers being mothers. That's the best way to get kids on the right track and reduce juvenile delinquency and gangs and violence. I don't have the answers to crime, but I can tell you more mothers at home is one good answer."

He added, "I'm convinced the jails are full of people who don't need to be there. Prisons should be mainly for the truly bad guys who commit violent crimes." This view parallels that of the more rational and astute criminologists and prison reformers, who believe a powerful, shadowy, profit-hungry "prison-industrial complex" combines with weak-kneed lawmakers, a fearful, brainwashed public, and media sensationalism to drive the costly, self-defeating prison craze in America. The prison budget in California now exceeds the outlay for the state's exceptional network of state-supported colleges. As noted, the term "prison-industrial complex" derives from Eisenhower's stern warning, as he bowed out after two terms as president, against the immensely powerful "military-industrial complex," which lobbies today at full throttle and has kept our so-called defense budget at a level approximately $10 billion higher than at the end of the Cold War.

Goldwater deplored the upsurge in crime in Arizona. "Crime is up in Phoenix, murders and serious stuff, and we didn't used to have any." The crux, of course, is that Phoenix today is a teeming urban center, not the more placid cow town of yore, when Barry was growing up.

It was the mean-spirited, dogmatic posturing at the 1992 GOP National Convention by both TV evangelist Rev. Pat Robertson, whom Goldwater considered a "money-grubber," and pseudojournalist/TV commentator/perennial presidential candidate Pat Buchanan that crippled the reelection campaign of President Bush and drove away many traditional, old-line conservatives like Goldwater and virtually all of the shrunken moderate wing of the GOP.

After Bill Clinton's election, Goldwater reminded me he'd said the religious right posed a serious threat to the future of the Republican Party. He had predicted President Bush would lose his bid for reelection if an antiabortion plank was inserted into the GOP platform, and that is what subsequently happened. In the presidential primaries of 2000, John McCain took up the

cudgels against the leadership of the religious right—
mainly Rev. Pat Robertson and Rev. Jerry Falwell—and
it probably resulted in his loss of the pivotal South Car-
olina primary. But Texas Governor George W. Bush, in
defeating McCain, embraced Robertson and Falwell
and their followers, and may find that to be a damning
albatross in his costly bid to succeed his father as
president.

As the imperious religious right tightened its grip
in the 1990s on the national GOP, Goldwater became
even more agitated and emphatic. When Republican
national chair Haley Barbour, a fox-sly good ole boy
from Mississippi, charged critics of the movement with
"religious bigotry" and "Christian-bashing," Goldwater erupted: "That's a crock. He's way the hell off base,
dead wrong. That religious bunch is crazy."

Goldwater was convinced that a radical right-wing
faction, large, tightly organized but widely dispersed,
and zealous, had "hijacked" the noble concept of historic conservatism and taken control of the Republican Party. They demonstrated their power in the first
Republican primaries of the twenty-first century and
voted overwhelmingly for Texas Governor Bush, thus

endorsing the GOP establishment choice and assuring the demise of the feisty maverick McCain, after a strong early showing.

"Isn't it interesting," mused moderate Republican Senator Mark Hatfield of Oregon, now retired, "how Barry lived long enough to see himself vindicated on a number of issues and was always highly respected for his integrity?"

Republican elder statesman Bob Dole confirmed in a letter last February, "Barry's legacy as the 'pioneer conservative' is secure."

Goldwater's evolving views as he entered the ranks of elder statesman attest emphatically to his character, devotion to principle, and willingness to accept certain realities that did not in his view conflict with or dilute the extent of his conservative ideals. He would never agree that abortion and homosexuality were truly conservative issues, but he stood unwavering in defense of such immutable principles as personal liberty and "equal justice under law" and other inalienable tenets of the American system.

Who he branded as the "neoconservatives" often were harsh and unforgiving in their criticism, dismissing him in the '90s as senile, dotty, and out of it, and pouring on other epithets.

He brushed off what he considered their "shallow" disapproval. He took sharp and vocal exception to the religious right and others who, in his view, hijacked and adopted conservatism as the rationale for their pet causes, with which Goldwater disagreed and which he believed corrupted the "purity" he espoused. He feared their rigidity and certainty that only they were right.

History, however, is likely to vindicate Goldwater as one who understood the unchanging fundamentals of the unique American experiment in self-government and had the courage to stand up and speak out in its defense and for its survival as the foundation of a living, thriving, free society.

Goldwater consistently demonstrated his uncommon faculty to separate the ephemeral from the enduring, his unwillingness to embrace as conservative whatever some zealots, oftentimes self-serving and superficial in their understanding, demanded. Conservatism as a philosophy swept across America in the final quarter of the twentieth century. Because of its popularity, loosely defined and often misunderstood, many have sought to fit their ideas, notions, agendas, and prejudices into an ever expanding box labeled "Conservative." This became a real hodgepodge, and Goldwater simply wasn't buying. He did not believe true conservatism could be twisted, bent, shaped, and/or altered to fit the whims and schemes of those he said don't understand its depth and true meaning.

The essence of Goldwater's cause was always "freedom," not merely in theory, but as it would apply to the life of each presumably free citizen of his country.

"To my mind, there is a cause. That cause is freedom. We stand in danger of losing that freedom," he said in his 1979 autobiography, titled, in the Goldwater manner, *With No Apologies*. It came straight from the shoulder and the heart, written by Barry himself from "the thousands of words which I dictated on the tape"—with some editorial "touching up" by the late Steve Shadegg, his great good friend and political confidant.

He did not see us losing freedom to "a foreign tyrant, but to those well-intentioned but misguided elitist utopians who stubbornly refuse to profit from the errors of the past."

He explained, "If I am right, if the Republic is in danger, then time is short. I must take this opportunity to share what I have seen and experienced as a member of the U.S. Senate, as my party's nominee for the presidency, as a man whose only aspiration has been to serve the cause of freedom. If I am wrong, time will display my error and reprimand me."

Times have changed dramatically in the past two decades. We live today in an era of opulence, with a rampaging stock market, technological wizardry, and material plenty for many. But millions of Americans do not share in the fruits, and many fight an endless battle merely to survive.

Goldwater's fight for freedom, to preserve and expand personal liberty, is as great a concern as it ever was. Rudyard Kipling asked the ultimate question: "What stands if Freedom fall?"

And Goldwater's cautionary warnings two decades ago in his autobiography are as valid today as then. In a letter to me on February 1, 2000, former President George Bush wrote simply, "Barry Goldwater was a man ahead of his times." And Goldwater's words confirm that observation:

Informed opinion is sharply divided. . . . We have
conjured up all manner of devils responsible for
our present discontent.
It is the unchecked bureaucracy in government.
It is the selfishness of multinational corporate giants.
It is the failure of the schools to teach and the
students to learn.
It is overpopulation.
It is wasteful extravagance.
It is squandering our natural resources.
It is racism.
It is capitalism.
It is our material affluence. . . .

Words that describe America today as accurately as
twenty years ago, when they were written, clear evidence that President Bush was perceptive in calling
Goldwater "ahead of his times."

The former senator continues:

When we scrape away the varnish of wealth, education, class, ethnic origin, parochial loyalties, we discover that however much we've changed the shape of
men's physical environment, man himself is still sinful, vain, greedy, ambitious, lustful, self-centered,
unrepentant, and requiring of restraint.

I cannot change what I am, nor would I wish to do so. I am quite aware of the risks in speaking frankly and candidly. My appraisal of the great figures of my time will certainly be challenged. I must question certain notions which have been authenticated by a vast amount of intellectual authority. My opinions . . . may once again make me a target of scorn and ridicule. . . . It is my ambition to share my experiences as I tried to establish a balanced authority, to maintain and support the ordered and just society. . . . Believing the American people possess the courage to face the truth and will find the strength to overcome the habits which threaten our destruction, I cannot keep silent.

Only Goldwater could—or would—have issued a warning so clear, cogent, discerning, so far "ahead of his times"—a phrase that might stand as his own fitting epitaph.

5

Friends, Fans, and Fence-Sitters View Goldwater with Warmth and Respect

Goldwater's career in the Senate will put him among the "giants" in the history of "the upper body."
—President Gerald Ford,
letter to author,
December 1996

Goldwater's staunch candor and straight talk earned him passionate fans and defenders among national leaders on both sides of the political aisle. There were detractors, too.

When Gerald Ford ran for election in 1976 after his appointment to succeed the disgraced Nixon, he was challenged by Ronald Reagan, Goldwater's eloquent TV spokesman in the failed presidential campaign of 1964. Goldwater's backing of Ford, who was "very grateful for this support in this close contest," was critical to Ford's nomination. But Goldwater's action offended many devout conservatives, including the Reagans, who felt that he "betrayed" Reagan, in part because he didn't want to surrender the mantle of "Mr. Conservative" and was jealous of Reagan's ascension.

That missed the point. Goldwater's notion of "loyalty" was quite different.

"Jerry Ford restored dignity and trust to the White House—when we needed it most—after Nixon's fall," he told me. Typically, Goldwater gave higher priority to the needs of the nation than to a "payback" for Reagan's "personal favor" to him in the 1964 campaign. The senator said Ford deserved the chance to "win his place" in the White House on his own. Goldwater was also convinced Ford would be the stronger candidate in November.

"I have always greatly admired Barry for his total frankness and dedication to his philosophical and political views," said former President Ford. "He never wavered under pressure from the news media or political opponents.

"Barry always said what he 'believed.' In August 1974, he publicly stated President Nixon should resign. . . . During his five-term service in the U.S. Senate, Barry was often an outspoken maverick who spoke with conviction, but was highly respected because of his candor. . . . Barry was an acknowledged expert on national defense issues and a forthright leader in America's superpower confrontation with the Soviet Union and its allies."

"Barry loved the United States Senate," said Bob Dole, former Senate leader from Kansas and GOP presidential standard-bearer in 1996 against Clinton, "and had many friends on both sides of the aisle. He was unique in many ways. He was independent, intelligent, irreverent, inspirational, and at times he could be irascible and unpredictable. I recall his comment that he might support a Democrat, Sam Nunn (senator from Georgia), for president." (Goldwater did, in fact, support a Democrat for Congress in Arizona, and she won handily, stirring an angry uproar among Republican leaders there.)

"Over the years," wrote Dole in a letter of February 1, 2000, "we were good friends, and his legacy as the 'pioneer conservative' is secure."

Well over on the far side of the aisle across from Dole and Ford was Senator Edward M. Kennedy, Democrat from Massachusetts, who nonetheless spoke highly of Goldwater the day after his death in 1998.

"I inherited my friendship and affection for Barry from my brothers (Senator Bobby and President JFK). They knew him and liked him, respected him in the Senate, and so did I. We often disagreed on particular issues, but our friendship transcended any disagreement.

"I think back to 1963, when President Kennedy was planning his reelection campaign for 1964. It was obvious that Barry was very likely to be the Republican nominee. My brother intended to debate him, and they talked of flying around the country together in a twentieth-century version of the Lincoln-Douglas debates."

That, of course, never happened, as Kennedy was struck down in Dallas by an assassin's bullets.

"Barry Goldwater never became president himself, but he laid the foundation for the presidency of Ronald Reagan," said Ted Kennedy. "Barry was a man of great courage and high principle. The Kennedys will miss him very much."

In a tough but fair appraisal of Goldwater, Walter Cronkite, for a half century America's "most trusted newsman," had this to say in February 2000:

"Barry Goldwater was, to the same persons at one time or another, the devil incarnate and a national hero. His intemperate speech accepting the presidential nomination at the 1964 Republican Convention shocked many in his own party. . . . In the very heat of the national debate that eventually would promise equal rights to African Americans, Goldwater did not even mention the matter in his acceptance speech. However, it was the very same forthrightness that made him a hero to the military in his prepolitical life and in his postpolitical life endeared him to many who once cringed at his words. In his declining retirement years he even seemed to embrace liberal causes, not the least was support of gays in the military and criticism of the Republican Party's tough stand against abortion."

Vintage Cronkite, as "Uncle Walter," in the manner of a great journalist, gave his balanced rendition of what he perceives as Goldwater's flaws and strengths.

Bruce DuMont, a journalist of a younger generation, founder and CEO of Chicago's Museum of Broadcast Communications and host of the nationally syndicated radio talk show "Beyond the Beltway," told me Goldwater "was my boyhood hero." DuMont attended the 1964 convention in San Francisco with his father.

"I cheered his every word at the Cow Palace. . . . The nonstop unfairness of the news media disgusted me. As an aspiring reporter, I vowed never to treat anybody the way the media treated Goldwater." At Goldwater's core, DuMont said after his death, "was a commitment to freedom, our most precious right. Goldwater abhorred snooty East Coast elitists, who encouraged government intervention into our lives, as well as holier-than-thou hypocrites of the religious right, who encouraged government intervention into our bedrooms. The cause of freedom lost its best friend last week, and I lost the best friend I never met."

U.S. Representative Jim Kolbe, another Republican congressman from Arizona, and former page for the senator, chuckled about angry attempts by some disgruntled Goldwater backers to take his name off GOP headquarters in Phoenix after he endorsed a woman Democrat for Congress.

"Barry Goldwater would be amused. . . . He was not one to be worried about names on a building. . . . It's typical of these people. If you're not with them 100 percent, you're not with them. Therefore, you're persona non grata. But that never kept Barry Goldwater from speaking his mind."

Kolbe also noted, "Both the party and the whole world around him changed, but I'm not sure he changed all that much."

In their positive appraisals of Goldwater, most political figures who knew him mention first his unvarying candor.

Former Senator Bill Bradley of New Jersey, a serious presidential aspirant in 2000, told me, "When I think of Barry, I think of candor—of someone who tells you exactly what he is thinking, in as direct a way as possible, and with an openness as wide as the vistas of Arizona."

Said retired Senator Paul Simon, the honorable Democrat from downstate Illinois, now heading the Public Policy Institute at Southern Illinois University, "He and I always had a good relationship because we were candid with each other. If there was one thing that was always true of Barry Goldwater, it was his candor. And that was refreshing."

General Colin Powell, a widely revered public figure, wrote, "I am a great fan of Barry." But he wasn't always. When he heard about Goldwater's vote against the Civil Rights Bill of 1964, the then young African American slapped a bumper sticker on his Volkswagen that said "All the Way with LBJ." Powell later got a different picture of Goldwater but admitted, "I didn't know him personally while he was in public life. During his years in Congress, I was a junior officer well off his radar screen."

In his later years, Goldwater was an unalloyed fan of Powell. "He's as knowledgeable as anybody in Washington today [in the mid-'90s]. If Colin had entered the race for president in '96, he would have been my first choice."

President George Bush saw Goldwater as "a man ahead of his times, who was a real inspiration to me in my early political days." Added President Bush, "Many of the things he was castigated for years ago are now in vogue. When you see people talking about privatizing part of Social Security, my mind goes back to what happened to Barry Goldwater in 1964 when he was derided for that very same view."

Even though Goldwater "disagreed almost violently with the political philosophy of the late Senator Hubert Humphrey," who lost the election for president to Nixon in 1968, he considered Humphrey "warm and wonderful, and, for the most part, very direct." They were experts at banter, but neither was mean or vindictive.

On one occasion, after a typically long-winded harangue by Humphrey, Goldwater suggested he'd "probably been vaccinated with a phonograph needle."

Humphrey instantly shot back: "Yes, and you would have been a great success in the movies working for Eighteenth Century Fox." They both roared.

After Goldwater's mild stroke in the fall of 1996, President Jimmy Carter wrote him on November 26: "Rosalynn and I were glad to learn of the progress you've made after your setback in September. We will keep you in our thoughts and prayers as you continue to regain your strength."

Carter added a handwritten P.S.: "I'm one of your great admirers, respecting you for your unquestioned honesty, truthfulness, and political courage." Carter signed it "J."

Even more eloquent and equally heartfelt was Ted Kennedy's tribute when Goldwater reached the end of his thirty years in the Senate, which were interrupted by his run for president. Kennedy and Goldwater had served together in the Senate for Barry's final three terms.

This is part of what he entered in the *Congressional Record* on October 17, 1986:

> Mr. President, I am proud to join my colleagues in this tribute to a man who for more than three decades has been one of the greatest institutions of the Senate and the nation. I am honored to call Barry Goldwater my friend. . . .
>
> We have had our differences on the issues, but as I have come to know him, I have been reminded again of an enduring truth. Friendship does not demand conformity of ideas—and mutual respect does not depend on an identity of ideology.
>
> All of us, Democrats as well as Republicans, know how Barry Goldwater stood his ground—and how the world finally came round to him. The choice he gave the nation has echoed across the years—and its reverberations can clearly be heard today in Ronald Reagan's speeches.

There is another, vital quality that marks him out. While Barry Goldwater takes issues seriously, he never takes himself too seriously. He is not self-important or self-righteous, and woe betide the partisan—of the Right or the Left—who runs afoul of Senator Goldwater by calling legitimate dissent unpatriotic, irreligious, or un-American.

He understands the essential nature of our national life—that the clock turns from the liberal to the conservative hour and back—again and again—and both traditions have something important to contribute. He fights fiercely for his tradition, but I have never heard him say a mean, personal, vindictive word about anyone on the other side of the debate. . . .

Most of all, Barry Goldwater comprehends that love of country transcends any particular policy or specific weapons system—that the values which always unite us as Americans are stronger than the views which sometimes divide us.

Finally, let me say that I speak not only for myself, but for two others who were honored to have him as a friend—John and Robert Kennedy. They swapped stories, teased each other, and vigorously debated everything from labor law reform to the nuclear test ban treaty. President Kennedy looked forward to Senator Goldwater's visits to the Oval Office. Robert

Kennedy shared his affection and concern for Native Americans—and prized his photographs of the West. I hope this doesn't get him in trouble with his other friends—but we like to think of Barry Goldwater as a Kennedy family friend.

In his final months in the White House in 1963, in a conversation with Ben Bradlee, President Kennedy said of Barry Goldwater: "I really like him—and if he's the Republican nominee and we're licked, at least it will be on the issues. At least the people will have a clear choice."

Today, two decades later, I can't help but reflect what a great debate it would have been—and what great friends they would have been afterwards.

Senator Goldwater has set a high standard. His life and service display the true and enduring meaning of "Duty, Honor, Country," and we shall miss him in this chamber.

Many a public figure has created die-hard foes in his home area, despite the affection of the majority. Thus, kind words from the dominant hometown newspaper are something to be treasured. These excerpts from an eloquent editorial in the *Arizona Republic* on the day of his death, May 28, 1998, have special meaning:

After ending a thirty-year Senate career in 1986, Barry Goldwater retired to his Paradise Valley hilltop home to cast down an occasional thunderbolt, more often than not at fellow Republicans, when the spirit moved him. . . .

The only certainty was that he'd win new affection from those who once regarded him as a lightweight, a lunatic, or worse, and that conservatives would gnash their teeth over the seeming loss of an icon.

Of course, they never lost him, because they had never owned him. First and last, Barry Goldwater was his own man.

By the time he died this morning, after the ravages of age and disease had driven him from the political scene he dominated for so long, many Arizonans had forgotten, or maybe never knew, the Goldwater who once was not an amusing eccentric but a politician of remarkable moral force and damn-the-torpedoes consistency. . . .

Yet, he remained, amid the calumny and adulation, a simple man of bemused humility who never quite understood what all the fuss was about. . . .

In an era before Medicare, interstate highways, Amtrak, enterprise zones, Superfunds, and affirmative action, even before emerging as the lion of conservatism, he understood, if only intuitively, the flaws lurking in a government that flaunted its unlimited capacity for goodness. And voters grasped the nuggets of truth in his eloquence. . . .

The truth is, Goldwater's forte was never legislative craftsmanship. . . . On the job, he was content to act as a sort of moral overseer, a finger in the dike against the onrushing tide of constitutional indifference, with only limited success and often to his electoral detriment. . . .

He was a man of intense loyalty, enduring friendships, absorbing distractions, and reckless candor. People sensed in him, whatever his political beliefs and cantankerous crustiness, a consummate decency and unspoiled authenticity—nothing more or less than what he seemed to be. . . . Barry Goldwater kept his powder dry and priorities straight. Arizona and America are better places for it. . . .

Following the onset of her husband's illness, Nancy Reagan sent this expression of their feeling for Goldwater:

"Barry started a crusade and handed the torch to Ronnie. Everybody's grateful for Barry and what he did for America. He has been a friend from the beginning and there will never be another Barry Goldwater."

The truthful observations of friends and foes and colleagues are a good way to gauge the worth and mettle of a man, and some of these comments provide a reasonable picture of the "real" Barry Goldwater.

To him, however, it was the praise, affection, trust, and support of ordinary people—the core of twenty-seven million who voted for him in 1964—that meant the most and formed the backbone of the conservative movement he launched.

6

Barry Surveys His Universe of Good and Not-So-Good Guys

He was a dishonest man who never told me the truth.
Lie after lie. I wouldn't trust him across that mountain.
—BG ON RICHARD NIXON,
TO AUTHOR, LOOKING OUT THE
WINDOW OF HIS LIVING ROOM,
PARADISE VALLEY, JULY 1994

BARRY GOLDWATER and Richard Nixon once were Republican comrades in arms. For some years, they were fairly close. But it all started to fall apart in the early 1960s and ended with a cataclysmic crash during the Watergate fiasco, which Goldwater brought to a merciful end by expediting Nixon's departure from the White House.

In 1960, Nixon, Ike's vice president for two terms, came within a hair's breadth of defeating John F. Kennedy for the presidency. It came down finally to tense combat in Illinois, where Kennedy was declared the victor by a scant seven-thousand-plus votes, which many felt were "manufactured" (call it "stolen") by the powerful machine of the late Mayor Richard J. Daley.

Nixon's Illinois brain trust, headed by often blustery business book publisher William Harrison Fetridge and soft-spoken but tough-as-nails Acme Steel chieftain Fred Gillies, huddled as the late returns trickled in, with prominent Washington attorney William P. Rogers, longtime Nixon confidant and later secretary of state. There were five or six others; I was the "kid" in the room, even though earlier in the year I had lost a close primary race for the Senate and was called in at the eleventh hour to try to shore up the faltering Nixon campaign.

Finally, in the wee hours, around 3 A.M. Wednesday, it became evident, even to the diehards in the small group, that Nixon had been counted out, whether fairly or fraudulently.

The elders were livid, having worked themselves into a frenzy of anger over what they believed was a stolen election. Their words were harsh and profane. They concluded that their only recourse was to go into court to obtain an injunction until the ballot count could be confirmed. The final outcome could be delayed for months, leaving the nation leaderless and vulnerable.

Bill Rogers suggested they call Nixon. From the first moment, the vice president was adamant. He was unalterably opposed to any legal action that would lead to uncertainty among the American people and throughout the world among U.S. allies and adversaries.

Under no circumstances, Nixon said, would he risk adverse action by our potential enemies while the state of the presidency was unsettled and governance in turmoil without an elected leader in place. This was a selfless side of Nixon that most people never saw, his unbending commitment to the best interests of the nation above his own. The notion of a lawsuit died there with his words in unmistakable opposition.

Nixon returned to California, bitter and depressed, to lick his wounds and plot his next move. It was neither astute nor wisely calculated.

Thrashing about, he impetuously decided to run for governor of California. For this quixotic move, he recruited George Christopher as his running mate for lieutenant governor. Christopher was the enormously popular mayor of San Francisco, the last Republican to hold that office. They were crushed in the general election, and Nixon bitterly told the press, "You won't have Nixon to kick around anymore."

Years later, in 1987, when I was publishing the *San Francisco Progress*, I told Christopher, who became a good friend, "If you'd been at the top of the ticket, George, you and Nixon would have won."

"Well, maybe," he responded, "but Dick had come so close to being president, and he asked me to run with him, and I felt he was entitled to the top spot."

After that defeat for a lesser office, it was widely assumed by everybody but Nixon that he was through politically. In 1964, however, Nixon tested the presidential waters against Goldwater, and he tilted surprisingly to the party's hitherto dominant liberal East Coast wing, formerly anathema to him, perhaps hoping the Rockefeller forces might turn to the former vice president if they couldn't agree on a candidate within their own ranks.

Goldwater was thoroughly disgusted by Nixon's maneuvering and derisively likened him to perennial candidate Harold Stassen, onetime "boy governor" of Minnesota.

But the final break came in 1973, when the Republican Party and the nation were reeling from the Watergate scandal. Goldwater was distressed. So were many colleagues.

Barry and Senator Charles H. (Chuck) Percy of Illinois were positioned at opposite ends of the Republican philosophical spectrum, Percy the acknowledged liberal, Goldwater the stout conservative. Both were ruggedly handsome, the casting director's version of the heroic American political leader. They weren't especially close personally, but they were soul mates in terms of unshakable integrity, two of the most decent men I've known in the political arena over several decades.

Percy said he knew Barry well "because we were the only senators who had formerly headed major businesses before entering politics. Mostly we were surrounded by lawyers." Percy was the "boy wonder" who at twenty-nine became president of camera-maker Bell & Howell in Chicago, while Barry ran the family department stores at a young age.

Both were deeply troubled by the spreading scandal of Watergate, which they saw inflicting great damage not only on their party but also on the trust of the nation in the integrity of the political process.

When President Nixon stated on television that he was unaware what his staff had done at Watergate, Percy went to Goldwater's office to suggest they take the initiative in seeking to resolve the dilemma. The two agonized over what to do and finally decided to seek a meeting with Nixon at the White House and urge him to "come clean."

The president received them in the California Room; in effect, they told him, "It is inconceivable that you did not know about the Watergate break-in." Nixon listened attentively but said nothing as they continued.

The two Republican "opposites" told Nixon he should acknowledge he knew about Watergate and in fact authorized the sleazy break-in.

They urged the president to "go on TV and confess to the American people, who are generous and forgiving," and added, "they would react well to your confession." If he followed their suggestion, they told him, they would publicly support his continuation as president despite growing pressure for him to leave the White House.

When they finished, Nixon spoke: "I can't possibly do that because I would be lying if I did. I did *not* know anything about it."

Without further talk, the two senators left.

When the tapes were revealed, Goldwater exploded in fury, knowing they had been lied to by the president. Goldwater never forgave Nixon, ultimately urged him to step down, and did not attend his funeral.

At his Arizona home in 1994, Goldwater revealed his lingering disappointment with Nixon: "I'm still pissed off at him. He was a dishonest man who never told me the truth. Lie after lie. I wouldn't trust him across that mountain," pointing to distant peaks.

His cold disdain for Nixon was untypical of Goldwater. He did not normally bear grudges. His flashes of anger passed. He had truly harsh words for very few of the political figures he encountered and knew over the years. The one thing he detested was blatant dishonesty. Lying was the worst sin, his mother impressed on Barry as a young boy, and this was the basis for his rupture with Nixon.

I heard him speak with utter disdain about only one other towering American politician. Mostly, he was forgiving and seldom meanly judgmental.

"LBJ made me sick," he told me. "Principle meant nothing to him. Every tough issue could be resolved by his wheeler-dealer style. Give 'em some pork in their state or let 'em have some special tax break for a big contributor."

After John Kennedy's death, Goldwater told Peggy, "I'm definitely not going to run. . . . The overwhelming reason . . . was my personal and political contempt for Lyndon Johnson. He was a master of manipulation. He solved tough public issues through private plotting. . . . Everything was a deal. . . . There would never be a battle of issues. . . . Johnson was a dirty fighter. Any campaign with him in it would involve a lot of innuendo and lies. . . . The man didn't believe half of what he said. He was a hypocrite, and it came through in the hollowness of his speech. . . . His only political dogma was expediency. . . . He never cleaned the crap off his boots. It trailed him from the Senate to the vice presidency and into the Oval Office itself. There's an old saying out in Arizona: If you get down in the manure, you come up smelling like it." This reflected the sometimes inelegant candor of Barry Goldwater.

Even though Goldwater was savaged mercilessly and unfairly by fellow Republicans Nelson Rockefeller and William Scranton, and other East Coast liberals, he didn't allow those campaign canards in the heat of the 1964 contest to fester over the years.

In his Senate office in 1983, Goldwater offered his perspective on his rocky relationship with Nelson. In their heyday, Goldwater and ebullient but tough four-term New York governor Rockefeller were viewed by press and public alike as bitter philosophical adversaries, the Arizona senator a passionate advocate of right-wing dogma, the New Yorker a flaming leftist by comparison.

"Not at all," Goldwater told me. "Our differences were probably not much more than an accident of birth, of environment, where we grew up and lived."

Goldwater clearly was shaped by his physical environment—rugged, barren Arizona, land of the sturdy, upright cacti rather than the leafy, billowing oaks, elms, and maples that abound and flourish in much of this nation.

Barry compared his pioneering, populist, entrepreneurial forebears, who reflected the western frontier and founded a department-store empire in then-virgin Arizona, with those of Rockefeller, born into a family of buccaneering capitalism, unlimited wealth and power, and social prestige.

"If Nelson had my Arizona upbringing, and I'd been raised by nannies on Park Avenue or one of those fancy estates instead of by a mother who could swear and shoot and drink with the best of them, and ruled the roost around home, things might have been a whole lot different.

"Guys like Nelson often turn liberal to ease their guilt over all that money," Goldwater chuckled.

But Barry did not harbor long-term rancor over Rockefeller's mean-minded abuse during the '64 campaign.

As for the patrician Scranton, whose staff tarred Goldwater relentlessly, often without Scranton's direct knowledge, Barry reminded me that the Pennsylvania governor was the first choice to be his vice presidential running mate, but that idea was vetoed unanimously by Goldwater intimates.

"I always liked Bill Scranton and thought his attacks were out of character," Barry said. Somewhat incongruously, Scranton, seemingly in a penitent mood, campaigned aggressively for Barry once he became the GOP nominee.

A decade later, in a rambling interview at his home for a *Chicago Tribune* feature article, I asked Barry for a candid size-up of other presidents he had known. Except for Nixon and Johnson, his comments were mainly gentle and generous.

Goldwater revered President Eisenhower, but his relationship with Ike was by no means always smooth. Goldwater felt Eisenhower, the career military commander and consummate hero of World War II, was "naive in politics."

In 1952, to the amazement of many Goldwater fans, the Arizona senator supported Eisenhower for the Republican presidential nomination over the conservative favorite, Senator Robert A. Taft of Ohio. This angered many hard-line GOP backers of Taft, about half of whom threatened to abandon future support of Goldwater. One of these was General Robert E. Wood, the brilliant, folksy chairman of Sears Roebuck, a confirmed isolationist and staunch right-winger.

Goldwater credited Ike's landslide victory over Adlai Stevenson with providing the "coattails" he needed to pull out his narrow first win for the Senate in the staunchly Democratic state of Arizona. In that election, Goldwater directly challenged "the union bosses," and, he said, "they never forgave me."

After Goldwater's first Senate speech, on May 12, 1953, a tough attack on federal price controls, President Eisenhower sent via an aide a three-word accolade, "Atta boy, Barry."

But it was inevitable the brash Senate newcomer would on occasion collide with Ike. Barry was distressed because the president was proposing to spend about $11 billion more in fiscal 1957 than in 1955, contrary to his pledge to reduce spending.

Goldwater teed off in a speech he delivered on April 8, 1957, "with the deepest sorrow," calling the Eisenhower program a "dime-store New Deal." It was, he said, "the largest peacetime budget in history." He realized, said Goldwater, that "attacking the proposal was a big risk," and he had "mixed emotions because my remarks criticized a friend."

Through the years, Ike and Barry generally got along well, and the president seemed to admire the outspoken westerner. After Barry's controversial, some said inflammatory, acceptance speech in 1964, Ike rebuffed pressure from Goldwater's Republican foes and maintained his promised neutrality.

Despite his deep-held philosophical convictions, which put him at odds with some of his Senate colleagues, Goldwater maintained close rapport and camaraderie with those of widely varying political persuasions, Republicans and Democrats alike, who ranged across the broad spectrum of political thought.

Most remarkable, perhaps, was his genuine affection and respect for the Kennedy clan, especially John F. Kennedy, whom he expected to challenge for the presidency in 1964, when JFK would be seeking a second term.

Barry looked forward to a vigorous race. "Jack and I were really good friends. We enjoyed each other's company, even though we disagreed on the big issues.

I enjoyed being around him, and I felt our competition for the White House would bring out our differences in a way that would be enlightening and give voters a real choice. Not like with LBJ."

As for the consummate liberal, Senator Hubert H. Humphrey, who was the Democratic nominee against Nixon in 1968, Goldwater said, "He was one of the most honorable men I have met in my life. . . . The day of Humphrey's funeral I was barely able to walk because of an operation, but I would not have stayed home even if I had to crawl. Hubert was a clean fighter. . . .

"I disagreed almost violently with the political philosophy of Hubert Humphrey. But he was warm and wonderful and, for the most part, a very direct man. . . . an agile, resourceful opponent . . . and never vindictive."

Goldwater had nothing but praise for Senator Sam Nunn, the now retired Georgia Democrat, with whom he teamed to pass the bitterly contested Pentagon reorganization measure they felt would help correct military blunders that led to disaster at Pearl Harbor.

"I placed absolute trust in Nunn. He never disappointed me, not once. With Sam, I'd take on the devil in hell."

Barry (right) is seen here as a youngster on the beach in 1911 with brother Bob (left) and sister Carolyn (center). They remained close siblings throughout their lives.

Baron Goldwater, Barry's dapper dad, with (from left) Bob, Carolyn, and Barry

A teenage Barry (right) with younger brother Bob and sister
Carolyn

Here Barry is with his mother, whom he adored and considered the most important influence in his life. Josephine (JoJo) Williams Goldwater came to Arizona from the tiny Mississippi River town of Bowen, Illinois.

Barry looks approvingly at one of thousands of model planes he built.

Barry rides down a Grand Canyon trail with friend Robert "Believe It or Not" Ripley.

The Goldwater clan

Barry roughing it with sons Barry Jr. (left) and Mike

Margaret (Peggy) Johnson Goldwater was Barry's wife for 51 years. She died in 1985.

Barry and Peggy stand outside their home, "Be-Nun-I-Kin," which is Navajo for "house on top of the hill." Goldwater built the home in Paradise Valley, Arizona, outside of Phoenix, in 1957–58.

"Shoot straight," Barry tells his son Mike in his gun room.

Radio pioneer Goldwater fiddles with his home station.

This charcoal drawing depicts (clockwise) Goldwater, campaign chief and longtime friend Dean Burch, and vice-presidential candidate Bill Miller at the 1964 Republican National Convention at the Cow Palace, San Francisco.
(Drawing by Franklin McMahon)

Goldwater and Richard Nixon share a light moment during Nixon's run for the presidency in 1960; Representative John Rhodes is at right.

Goldwater and Vice President Richard Nixon discuss campaign strategy in 1960.

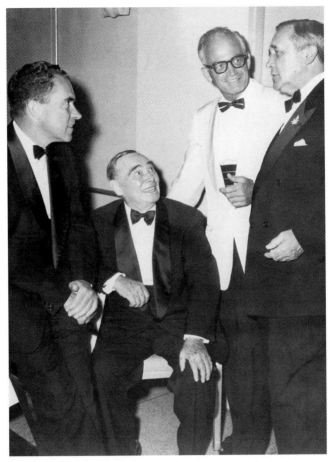

Barry Goldwater wears a tropical tuxedo at a black-tie fund-raiser for Richard Nixon's 1960 presidential campaign.

Barry Goldwater has the attention of Republican heavyweights; from left, Gerald Ford, Barry Goldwater, Everett Dirksen, Dwight D. Eisenhower, Leslie Arends, Richard Nixon, and Thomas E. Dewey.

Goldwater in 1964 with his vice-presidential running mate, Bill Miller, Republican representative from New York

Author Bill Rentschler (left) at the Rockford, Illinois, airport while on the senate campaign trail in 1970 with Barry Goldwater and *Rockford Register Republic* publisher William K. Todd.

(Photo courtesy of the author)

Senator Goldwater, Representative John Rhodes from Arizona (left), and Senator Hugh Scott from Pennsylvania meet the press after they told President Nixon he could not survive in office after Watergate. Within hours, Nixon resigned.

Goldwater and Ford have an intimate moment at the White House after Jimmy Carter defeated Ford in the 1976 election.

President Ronald Reagan presents Goldwater with a medal in 1982 for serving five senate terms.

First Lady Nancy Reagan beams at Barry; President Reagan is in the background, 1986.

After thirty years of distinguished service in the U.S. Senate, Goldwater was succeeded in 1987 by then Representative John McCain.

(Photo courtesy of John McCain)

Barry and Susan pose for a photo in 1994. Susan was Barry's second wife; they were married in 1992.

(Photo courtesy of Susan Goldwater)

First Lady Hillary Rodham Clinton visits Barry and his wife, Susan, in October 1996 at their Paradise Valley home after Barry suffered his first stroke.

(Photo courtesy of Susan Goldwater)

Barry gets a visit from President Bill Clinton along with Barry's wife, Susan, son Michael, and his doctor while recuperating in the hospital, in 1996.

(Official White House photograph)

Beloved American artist Norman Rockwell painted this portrait around the time Goldwater was a presidential candidate.

Goldwater regarded working with Nunn to pass the defense reorganization bill as the highlight of his thirty-year Senate career. Barry even considered supporting the Democrat senator for president.

During an interview in 1994, I also asked for his capsule appraisals of living U.S. presidents.

How about Jimmy Carter? He leaned back and chuckled softly.

"You know, the longer he's out of office, the better he looks. Every president thinks he sits at the right hand of God. But Carter is probably closer than the rest of 'em. A good man."

Ronald Reagan gained enormous credibility and became a plausible presidential contender when he articulated the conservative credo for Goldwater on national TV during that ill-fated 1964 campaign. Goldwater, however, was cautious in his assessment of the former actor and two-term president:

"We'll have to wait fifty years for the historians to tell us how well he did by the country. I personally think he did a good job. He was not very knowledgeable, but he absorbed information very quickly. He could come into a room completely ignorant of the subject, but after about five or ten minutes, he could join in and give a good account of himself. And what a convincing speaker he was!"

Goldwater admired President Ford. "Jerry Ford," Goldwater recalled, "restored dignity and trust to the White House—when we needed it most—after Nixon's fall. A thoroughly decent fellow, Ford."

On George Bush: "I like him. I have great respect for him. A nice gentleman. But he was never the equal of his father (the late U.S. Senator Prescott Bush, Connecticut Republican, with whom Goldwater served). George never had a clear vision of what he wanted to do as president, and I don't think he really had the stomach for a second term."

When Vice President Spiro Agnew was forced out, Goldwater told President Nixon, "My personal choice would be George Bush." Goldwater described Bush's 1992 campaign for reelection against Bill Clinton as "the worst-run campaign I've ever seen, on a par with the Mike Dukakis campaign four years earlier."

How about Clinton?

"He's very articulate, with a good brain. He doesn't know much about foreign policy, but he's a quick learner. I'm not at all sure he can win in '96. He's got too much to do to get his ass out of the mud. We Republicans have a good shot."

Who'd make the best Republican candidate?

"Everybody asks me that. I'm not sure. It's still early. Maybe Jack Kemp (the former pro quarterback who ran for vice president with Dole). Dick Cheney (former secretary of defense under Reagan) might be the best man, but he's had two heart attacks. Frankly, I don't think Bob Dole can win. I like him, but he's got a negative image and kind of a mean streak."

When I asked him, Goldwater couldn't name a single private-sector CEO for whom he had high regard. "There are damn few out there today who are leaders. When they get in trouble, they chop people off the payroll. That's not leadership."

How about Ross Perot? "If I had a government in trouble, I sure wouldn't call Perot. If I had a business in trouble, I probably would."

The former senator voiced his most extravagant accolades for former British Prime Minister Margaret Thatcher.

"Now there's a helluva gal. She's one of the greatest women who ever lived." He added, "She should have been a man," a remark calculated to win him no plaudits from avid feminists, which troubled him not at all. "They can think what they want."

In recalling political people he's known in his long career, Barry Goldwater in no instance strayed from the candor that marked his lifelong demeanor.

7

Shameful Media Blitz "Nukes" Barry in 1964

*It was the distortions I couldn't overcome.
That media bunch put horns on me, made me into
a zealot. That's not Barry Goldwater.*

—BG TO AUTHOR, INTERVIEW AT
HIS PARADISE VALLEY HOME,
JULY 1994

IT WAS HARDLY THEIR FINEST HOUR. Far from it.

The big-time media—press and TV alike—did not by any stretch distinguish themselves in the presidential campaign of 1964. In retrospect, all but a handful of journalism's superstars and influential organs of opinion roundly embarrassed themselves—if truth is to be a prime measuring stick of media performance.

Probably no influential American critical to the history of the twentieth century was so savagely and thoroughly misrepresented and widely caricatured as Barry Goldwater in that campaign.

The media were mainly the conduit. They took at face value with little reflection or tough questions the mean-minded pap fed them by the Nelson Rockefeller and Lyndon Johnson forces. They simply regurgitated the press releases, self-serving statements, and vicious put-downs. These were published and broadcast almost promiscuously because so many on the media firing line and in top editorial positions tended to agree with the wrongful portrayals of Goldwater. Some of the best-known and widely acclaimed columnists and pundits were the worst offenders.

Looking back from today, David Brooks, who writes for the *Weekly Standard*, said, "Goldwater was treated as a bizarre menace by much of the American press corps. But when he died in May (1998), you would have thought it was Eleanor Roosevelt breathing her last, the way some of the liberal pundits carried on."

Rockefeller, governor of New York, frequently mentioned as a virtual heir apparent to the presidency, scion of power and wealth, had put together the best public-relations machine money could buy. His minions couldn't always deliver everything Rocky wanted for himself, but their attack skills were finely honed, and Barry Goldwater was their sole target in 1963–64. They succeeded in transforming the normally amiable, straight-shooting son of the New West into a fearsome creature who would incinerate U.S. foes, dismantle Social Security, and wreak havoc on innocents as president, and they handed over to LBJ the ultimate game plan for his electoral rout. Goldwater must be stopped, even destroyed. "They made me into a grotesque monster," lamented Barry.

He was at times distraught over the relentless distortions.

Moderate Republican Senator Mark O. Hatfield of Oregon, his colleague and friend, told me, "Antoinette [Hatfield's wife] and I were accompanying Barry back to the airport following a 1964 rally in Portland, where I had introduced the senator. The news at that time was not encouraging.

"Senator Goldwater turned to us and said, 'How did I get myself into this situation? I must have had a hole in my head.'"

Goldwater said in his 1979 autobiography that the media were reasonably tolerant of him as one among 100 senators, but "the possibility of a conservative

Goldwater presidency was anathema to the lords of the media. . . . Many observers, troubled by the unanimity of action on the part of the eastern press, perceived it to be some sort of sinister conspiracy."

He singled out some of the worst offenders: venerated Walter Lippman, widely alluded to as a nonpareil among journalists; respected columnist Joseph Alsop; TV's Howard K. Smith; the *New York Times*; the *Washington Post*; the now defunct *New York Herald-Tribune*; and the *Los Angeles Times*. He was convinced that rank-and-file political reporters, inclined in any event to the liberal line, largely aped the big names of the news business in framing their anti-Goldwater coverage.

As a journalist myself, I've always felt that it made sense to view with skepticism the self-serving stuff of candidate PR releases. Better, more high-minded newspeople generally make it a point to verify and check out claims and charges made by any politician's hired hands.

Arthur Hays Sulzberger, late publisher of the venerated *New York Times*, issued this sound and balanced admonition in 1948:

"Obviously, a man's judgment cannot be better than the information on which he has based it. Give him the truth and he may still go wrong when he has the chance to be right, but give him no news or present him only with distorted and incomplete data . . . and you destroy his whole reasoning processes and make him something less than a man."

In that 1964 campaign, the mainstream press, including Sulzberger's *Times*, paid little heed to his words, and the distortions destroyed the "whole reasoning processes" of the voting public, turning Goldwater into something he was not.

John S. Knight, publisher of the old *Chicago Daily News* and *Akron Beacon Journal*, and a genuine lion of journalism in that era and beyond, was so appalled and fed up with the distortions and attacks on Goldwater that he wrote in one of his famous Saturday editorials in June 1964:

> I can no longer stand silently by and watch the shabby treatment Goldwater is getting from most of the news media. . . . Of the syndicated columnists I can think of, there are only a few who are not savagely cutting down Senator Goldwater day after day.
>
> Some of the TV commentators discuss Goldwater with evident disdain and contempt. Editorial cartoonists portray him as belonging to the Neanderthal

Age or as a relic of the nineteenth century. It is the fashion of editorial writers to persuade themselves that Goldwater's followers are either kooks or John Birchers. This simply isn't so. The Goldwater movement represents a mass protest by conservatively minded people against foreign aid, excessive welfare, high taxes, foreign policy, and the concentration of power in the federal government.

Goldwater said he greatly enjoyed years later reading Knight's eloquent defense of him, but "it didn't do much at the time to dissuade most of the rascals who delighted in tearing me down."

What seemed a coordinated chorus of near hateful rhetoric commenced as San Francisco drew near. Goldwater said in his autobiography, "I lost whatever small chance I ever had to be president . . . at the Republican National Convention." A combination of Rockefeller Republicans and media antagonists had "nuked" Goldwater.

An interview with ABC's Howard K. Smith was twisted to suggest that Goldwater would use nuclear bombs to win the war in Vietnam. What Goldwater said in the interview, in response to a question by

Smith, was this: "There have been several suggestions made. I don't think we would use any of them, but defoliation of the forest by low-yield atomic devices could well be done. When you remove the foliage, you remove the cover [for enemy troops]."

He explained, "I didn't suggest we should use the atomic bomb in South Vietnam. I said there had been several suggestions made. I knew the military had discussed the possibility of using toxic defoliants as well as atomic artillery shells extremely low in radiation. I qualified my response by saying, 'I don't think we would use any of them.'"

In advance of the Smith broadcast, both AP and UPI released stories suggesting Goldwater advocated the use of nuclear weapons in Vietnam. UPI later retracted its story, but the retraction, Goldwater said, "never caught up with the Sunday-morning headlines. It was a near-fatal blow." What it did was link Goldwater wrongly with the advocacy of nuclear warfare, and it gave his enemies a deadly weapon to use against him.

The *New York Herald-Tribune*'s Joseph Alsop distorted Goldwater's response to Howard K. Smith in this way in his July 6 column: "In the course of [the

TV interview with Smith], the senator *blithely* suggested nuclear defoliation as one possible way to win the Vietnamese War."

Soon thereafter, Walter Lippman, also in the *Herald-Tribune*, wrote: "In foreign affairs Goldwater is ready to confront the Soviet Union and China with a choice between capitulation and war." Goldwater, sagging from the assault, cited this from fellow Republican Henry Cabot Lodge, who ran for vice president with Nixon in 1960: "We must never countenance such a thing as a trigger-happy foreign policy which would negate everything we stand for and destroy everything we hope for."

One of the lowest blows came from C. L. Sulzberger, another member of the *New York Times*'s ruling family, who wrote without ever meeting or interviewing Goldwater: "The possibility exists that, should he enter the White House, there might not be a day after tomorrow."

The *St. Louis Post-Dispatch*, owned by the Pulitzer family and a respected gem of midwestern journalism, weighed in with this distorted description of the Goldwater forces: "A coalition of Southern racists, county-seat conservatives, desert rightist radicals, and suburban backlashers."

The dean of political cartoonists, pen name Herblock, of the *Washington Post*, drew a caricature of Goldwater emerging from a sewer and telling a poor, frightened, and freezing young girl, huddled in a doorway with her baby, "Why don't you go out and inherit a department store?" The syndicated cartoon ran in papers from coast to coast.

Yet another obscene "hit" was a purported "psychological study" published in a long-gone magazine called *Fact*, which claimed that 1,846 psychiatrists across the country decided without any exam or case history that Goldwater was not "psychologically fit" to be president. The respondents were not required to sign their names, but the press eagerly picked up on the results, and the *New York Times* ran a paid full-page ad touting the survey.

In response, the president and medical director of the American Psychiatric Association wrote in a joint letter for the general public: "By attaching the stigma of extreme political partisanship to the psychiatric profession as a whole in the heated climate of the current political campaign, *Fact* has in effect administered a low blow to all who would advance the treatment and care of the mentally ill of America." Goldwater later sued the magazine for libel and won a money judgment.

Then, on July 12, the very eve of the convention, presumed Goldwater friend Bill Scranton released a four-page letter addressed "Dear Senator"—with "Sincerely yours, William W. Scranton" typed at the bottom, but unsigned.

Goldwater was nonplussed.

"I put the letter down," he said. "My first thought was to send the letter back to Scranton with a note suggesting that someone typed his signature to a letter it would have been impossible for him to write."

That turned out to be correct. Scranton had not read the letter, which was put together by two gung-ho aides, before it was hand-delivered to Goldwater.

"We decided to release copies . . . to every delegate," Goldwater said. "I gave a copy to the press with a simple statement saying I couldn't believe my old friend Bill Scranton had written such a letter or intended the language to be so violent. . . .

"I told [two close associates] that if I had done any of the things Scranton had charged me with doing, that if I held any of the beliefs he attributed to me, I wouldn't vote for myself, and Peggy wouldn't vote for me either."

The contents of the letter were devastating and outlined in an orderly manner the specious charges made against Goldwater by his GOP attackers, bent on destroying this grave threat to their longtime rule of the party.

These were the charges leveled in the Scranton letter:

You have too often casually prescribed nuclear war as a solution to a troubled world.

"I read that sentence twice," said Goldwater. "Never once in all my statements or my writings on foreign policy had I ever advocated nuclear war as a solution to a troubled world. I have never believed the security interests of the United States required us to destroy communist Russia. . . . This charge wasn't being leveled by some pacifist, left-wing radical; this total distortion of my search for peace was coming from a fellow Republican."

You have too often allowed the radical extremists to use you.

"Where? When? Who? How? I asked myself."

You have too often stood for irresponsibility in the serious question of racial holocaust.

"I had voted for every civil rights measure except for the one in June (Civil Rights Act of 1964), and my objections to that piece of legislation were on very solid constitutional ground." The charge that Goldwater was racist upset the senator more than any other, because it impugned his personal views on the dignity and worth of every citizen in a free society.

You have too often read Taft and Eisenhower and Lincoln out of the Republican Party.

"At that point I had to wonder if Bill Scranton had taken leave of his senses."

In the wake of that inflammatory letter, Nelson Rockefeller on the convention floor went to extreme lengths to bury Goldwater without mentioning his name:

Precisely one year ago today, on July 14, 1963, I warned that the Republican Party is in real danger of subversion by a radical, well-financed, highly organized minority, wholly alien to the sound and honest conservatism that has firmly based the Republican Party in the best of its centuries' traditions. . . . The methods of these extremist elements I have experienced at firsthand. Their tactics have ranged from cancellation of a speaking engagement before a college, to outright threats of personal violence. . . . I can personally testify to their existence, and so can countless others who have also experienced anonymous midnight and early-morning telephone calls, unsigned and threatening letters, smear and hate literature, strongarm and goon tactics, bomb threats and bombings, infiltration and takeover of established political organizations by Communist and Nazi methods—these extremists feed on fear, hate, and terror. They have no program for America, no program for the Republican Party, no program to keep the peace and bring freedom to the world.

"Is it any wonder," Goldwater asked almost plaintively, "the voters were learning to fear a Goldwater presidency?"

All this was grist for the salivating media, giving Goldwater's chief detractors confirmation that they were right all along.

"The newspaper reports and television commentators covering the San Francisco convention provided the nation with a bleak, almost frightening picture of a ruthless Goldwater machine crushing opponents, denying anyone who disagreed with us the right to speak, and somehow dishonoring the process by which parties select their presidential nominee," said Goldwater. "I couldn't believe they were talking about me."

As an elected Goldwater delegate from Illinois, said to be the youngest in the nation, or close to it, I was shocked by this distorted media portrayal of the Goldwater methods and mien. I viewed the senator as a man of rare integrity in a soiled political climate. I was honored to represent him. Even though he was somewhat more conservative, I felt he represented a standard that the nation could embrace with pride and confidence. As a fledgling journalist, I was appalled by the words of some of my media role models. I was equally upset by the actions of the Rockefeller Republicans, several of whom I had greatly respected up to that point.

There were journalists, such as John Knight, who perceived the unfairness of many colleagues and stood up for Goldwater.

Other notable examples were David Lawrence, syndicated columnist and editor-founder of *U.S. News and World Report*, and Arthur Krock, senior political writer for the *New York Times*, who defended Goldwater against widespread charges that he was a racist. As cited previously, more than any other charge made against him, the one branding him a racial bigot angered and disturbed him most. His whole life history rebutted that notion. Years earlier, he had integrated the Goldwater stores, as well as the military unit he commanded. He was personally close to and thought to be a champion for many of the Native Americans in Arizona. This was only a small part of the overall picture of his sensitivity to minority rights.

Before he voted against the 1964 Civil Rights Act, Goldwater told his fellow senators: "I am unalterably opposed to discrimination of any sort." But he further explained that he could not support a law whose provisions "fly in the face of the Constitution, and which require for their effective execution the creation of a police state." The measure was considered a historic breakthrough, made possible by a coalition headed by then Senate majority leader Lyndon Johnson and Republican minority leader Everett McKinley Dirksen, the earthy plainsman from Illinois who later nominated Goldwater, "a peddler's grandson," for president of the United States, and who earlier had made a trip to Arizona to urge Barry to make his first run for the U.S. Senate.

In terms of dirty campaigning, Goldwater was infuriated by two TV commercials run by the Johnson campaign and contrived by top Johnson aide Bill Moyers in concert with the high-powered Doyle Dane Bernbach New York advertising agency. Moyers is portrayed today by the media as philosophical, even-handed, and near saintly. Yet, the commercials he helped create belied that image. One depicted Goldwater's hands—without showing his face and body—tearing into bits a Social Security card, symbolizing his intent to destroy Social Security, which was entirely without basis in fact.

Far more deadly was the second commercial, which made Goldwater seem, in his words, "a mad nuclear bomber." In this spot, a little girl in a sun-kissed field of daisies was shown plucking petals from a flower. In the background, a male voice starts a countdown— ten . . . nine . . . eight . . . becoming increasingly louder. Then comes an explosion, and the little girl is swallowed up in a mushroom cloud. The voice makes a pitch for electing LBJ, never mentioning Barry Goldwater: "These are the stakes: To make a world in which all of God's children can live, or go into the dark. We must either love each other, or we must die. Vote for President Johnson on November third. The stakes are too high for you to stay home."

In other words, by Goldwater's reading, "Barry Goldwater would blow up the world if he became president of the United States."

It was a vicious, irresponsible commercial that delivered an indefensible message. To his dying day, Goldwater, who bore few grudges, never forgave Moyers—or Johnson, who OK'd the commercial. "The ad," he said, "was a repellent lie."

He confided, "Every time I see Moyers on TV, I get sick to my stomach and want to throw up. He's a sanctimonious phony. I consider him the father of the negative campaign ads which have brought politics to such low repute today."

I can't help wondering how Bill Moyers, darling of the media and some intellectuals, would explain and justify that ad today.

The nuclear ad apparently ran just once for pay, but it was rerun dozens of times on news and other TV shows. The ad triggered outrage among Goldwater backers and some sophisticates, but it terrified many of the general public.

Said columnist James (Scotty) Reston of the *New York Times*, who was at times as outspoken and acerbic as Goldwater, "I wish the media had kicked the stuffing out of LBJ and the White House on the TV ads issue. I think the senator is absolutely right in saying the press was remiss in letting that garbage get out without nailing them. It was outrageous—no doubt about it. He's got a legitimate gripe."

The *Washington Post*'s Ben Bradlee, who as editor orchestrated his paper's Watergate coverage a decade later, described the Moyers bomb ad as "a fucking outrage."

David Broder, also of the *Post*, long one of the more respected, fair-minded syndicated columnists, wrote:

"The media's original perception of Goldwater was fundamentally false. He was not the crazy madman that some depicted. However, some substantial criticism was justified. He made some mistakes and misstatements that we reported as facts.

"The media have a tendency to characterize men and events and oversimplify them. We presented a scary picture of Goldwater. It was not the whole cloth of the man and politician. Our characterization of him as an extremist was a terrible distortion."

There was a presidential race yet to be run, but Barry Goldwater knew it was not one he could win.

8

How the Power of Twisted Words Doomed Goldwater

I would remind you that extremism in the defense of liberty is no vice. And let me remind you also that moderation in the defense of justice is no virtue.
— BG ACCEPTANCE SPEECH,
COW PALACE, SAN FRANCISCO,
JULY 17, 1964

THERE WAS ELECTRICITY in the air as the Goldwater forces converged on San Francisco, grimly determined to wrest control of the Republican Party from the big-money, "country-club," East Coast liberals who had dominated for so long. Barry's backers were messianic in their belief that the Goldwater crusade would deliver them from a certain bondage and open the way for the inclusion of the New West, new leadership, and a new commitment to bedrock conservative principles.

Fresh-faced teenagers togged out in colorful banners, sashes, billowy skirts, straw hats, and big AuH_2O buttons, my oldest daughter, Sarah, among them, skittered like waterbugs about the hotel lobbies, chattering breathlessly in high-pitched voices and singing paeans of praise for their candidate.

Little clusters of their adult counterparts spoke more guardedly but with much the same intensity as they contemplated the fruits of their intensive labors back home.

Barry Goldwater had in tow the delegates needed for the nomination when he arrived in San Francisco. But his adversaries within his own party, led by Nelson Rockefeller, Henry Cabot Lodge, William Scranton, George Romney, and other members of the "Stop Goldwater" cabal, with their vitriolic pounding, virtually assured the resounding victory of Lyndon Johnson in the fall.

"The press played a strong supporting role," Goldwater said, "but for the most part it functioned as a carrier of the destructive statements, devastating personal criticism, and outright falsehoods of my fellow Republicans.

"By the time the convention opened, I had been branded as a fascist, a racist, a trigger-happy warmonger, a nuclear madman, and the candidate who couldn't win. At the time, a number of observers remarked that throughout the campaign, and particularly in San Francisco, my manner was brusque, unfriendly. Perhaps it was. It isn't easy to be cheerful, charitable, and forgiving when comrades from your earlier battles are thrusting their bayonets into your back."

So Goldwater, in what should have been a time of exhilaration and triumph, was confronted by a band of spoilsports who would take much of the joy and promise out of the historic event, perhaps from conviction but more likely because a Goldwater presidency would dash their own lofty ambitions.

There was no way Goldwater could be denied the nomination. He had the delegates in hand to ensure his convention victory. But the rancor that permeated the entire atmosphere assured the devastating beating that would come in November.

Among Republicans in Illinois, based on my race for the Senate in 1960, I was known as a moderate, more liberal than Barry on social issues but conservative on most fiscal matters. I went to San Francisco as an elected Goldwater delegate with high hopes and unbounded respect for the integrity and free-thinking, maverick ways of my candidate.

There was an unexpected highlight of my train ride to San Francisco. As we rocked and rolled through the variegated countryside of America, there came a tap on our bedroom door: "The president wonders if you'd come back for a visit."

I was befuddled, my mind immediately flashing to President Kennedy, who certainly wouldn't be on this train en route to the Republican National Convention. Of course not.

I followed the messenger to the last car on the train and found President Dwight David Eisenhower intent on draining a putt on a green carpet in his private car.

He straightened up, flashed that huge, warming grin, his face pink and cherubic, and welcomed me to his sanctum. First he introduced me to former First Lady Mamie and then to her friend Mrs. John Hilson, whose son I'd known in college.

Back in 1960, when Ike came to Chicago for the prior national convention which nominated Nixon, his vice president, to run against Kennedy, it was his swan song after eight years of "good feeling" during his presidency. The Illinois GOP was eager to give him a rousing farewell, and I was asked by state chairman Victor Smith to lead the tribute to Ike.

I concluded that General Ike had been treated to his share of twenty-one-gun salutes, so I came up with an alternative: a twenty-one-*person* salute during which he'd be greeted by a diverse mix of twenty-one Illinoisians, ranging from "Mr. Cub" Ernie Banks to Dr. Julius Hovany, a Hungarian-language newspaper publisher, as he disembarked from Air Force One. That was the highlight of what we called "Thank You, Ike Day," and he was genuinely touched. I guess that's the main reason he invited me back for a visit that interrupted his golf.

We talked for ten minutes or so, and the former president praised "my good friend Barry" for his candor, courage, and good judgment. "We didn't always see eye to eye, but I knew Barry would always tell it as he saw it, and I trusted him implicitly," said Ike. He expressed concern about the division in the party and said he hoped things could be "resolved short of a floor fight."

He asked graciously about my children, two of whom, Peter and Mary, he had met at the airport, and

I was pleased to report they were thriving. That was a happy, exciting interlude before we arrived for the main event.

On June 1, in New York, General Eisenhower held a press conference. He told covering reporters, "You people tried to read Goldwater out of the party; I didn't." Despite intense heat from longtime friends and allies, as well as media moguls, Ike maintained his promised neutrality in the presidential contest and thus protected Goldwater's big lead.

It was difficult for me to understand the bitter antagonism of Goldwater's party foes, who seemed willing to risk certain disaster for their own seemingly selfish ends. I knew Rocky a bit, found him outgoing and engaging, and we had a cordial relationship. In 1959, he offered to support me for National Young Republican chairman if I would back out of the Senate primary in Illinois, more of a favor to his friend Illinois Governor William G. Stratton than to me. I declined. In his attacks on the upstart Goldwater, he seemed oblivious to any team-play concept and adopted a haughty, "to-the-manor-born" attitude.

Goldwater's appearance before the Platform Committee, chaired by brainy, highly regarded Wisconsin congressman Melvin Laird, was especially revealing in assessing the Arizonan's demeanor and sincerity in seeking unity and good feeling:

> I will not presume to tell you what should go into this platform in terms of specific planks or programs. You are Republicans. You know our Republican record. You know where we stand in Congress. You know the programs we've created and fought for. You know the ones we have resisted. You know where we have disagreed on this or that detail, but most important, you know the great basic principles on which we agree. Let those meaningful principles guide your minds and hearts and reject the temptation to make this party's platform a bandstand for any factional cause. You must seek a document that will unite us on principle and not divide us. . . . We have come here to cross the great bridge from weary, futile, and fatuous [Democratic] leadership in national administration, to strong, active, and hopeful leadership, and you must take the first step.

Does that sound in any way like the rantings of a wild-eyed extremist or party-wrecking egotist?

Goldwater explained that his words originated with the temper of the Constitutional Convention in Philadelphia nearly two centuries earlier. The delegates were at an impasse, and, in that hour of crisis, George Washington offered this advice: "If to please the people, we offer what we ourselves disapprove, how can we afterwards defend our work? Let us raise a standard to which the wise and honest can repair. The event is in the hands of God."

Goldwater said he could "find no better words to express my innermost feelings about the issues to be decided in San Francisco. I knew we had made mistakes. I had provided my enemies with numerous opportunities to attack me by failing to be rigidly specific on all my recommendations. . . . I truly believed that if the American voters could be provided an opportunity to understand the real difference between what we would do as Republicans and what the other party offered, our cause would prevail."

Goldwater said the platform drafted under the supervision of Mel Laird was "generally satisfactory to me, but I had not controlled its writing." Actually, that was quite unusual, for presidential nominees generally dictated the outlines of the platform that would then serve as a blueprint for their campaign stance on key issues.

On Wednesday evening of the convention, the names of Barry Goldwater and seven others were placed in nomination: William Scranton, Nelson Rockefeller, Henry Cabot Lodge, George Romney, Senator Hiram Fong of Hawaii, U.S. Representative Walter Judd of Minnesota, and Senator Margaret Chase Smith of Maine. Most of these were more or less ceremonial and balm to egos, since the die was cast.

On the first ballot, Goldwater received more votes than any candidate in either party had ever received on the first ballot of a contested convention where the roll call continued uninterrupted to the end without allowing any state to change its vote. Goldwater garnered 883 out of 1,308—more than twice as many as the combined first-ballot votes of all other candidates.

Despite this overwhelming delegate support, polls were showing Goldwater as an 80–20 loser to Lyndon Johnson. The reasons given by voters for this shocking rejection of the party's certain nominee reflected the charges leveled by his Republican opponents.

"I was an extremist. I was a hawk who would get us into war. I would abolish Social Security. I was anti–civil rights. I was opposed to farm subsidies. I disapproved of such government subsidies as the TVA (Tennessee Valley Authority). I was antilabor.

"Only a few of those polled were outright supporters of Lyndon Johnson. They preferred the president because *they were afraid of me.*"

Afraid of Barry Goldwater—described for me by Walter Cronkite as someone who at different times was perceived by the same persons as "the devil incarnate and a national hero." Afraid of Goldwater. Which shows how media power can shape and distort the true personas of candidates—then, almost a half century ago, and now, in the presidential campaign of 2000.

Barry Goldwater's moment of triumph on the convention stage thus was soiled and savaged by the grating clamor raised by his detractors.

When the convention, marred by that rancor, finally bestowed its prize on Goldwater, there came the prime example of the power of words, how they can be twisted to obscure their real meaning, how words can move a nation. There were the powerful words of President Franklin D. Roosevelt in wartime, of Winston Churchill in stalwart defense of his tiny island, of Martin Luther King in sharing his dream, of Adolf Hitler in fomenting hatred and nationalistic excess, of John F. Kennedy in his stirring inaugural speech.

A mere thirty passionate words from Barry Goldwater's acceptance speech in San Francisco ultimately sealed his undoing and the cornerstone of his resounding defeat. Their resonance wrongly brought to mind all the specious charges against him and wrongly added to his impossible burden. What he said—and his words echoed from the capacious Cow Palace to the ears of those whose aim was to bury him, and whose interpretation, in my view, was wholly wrong—was this: "I would remind you that extremism in the defense of liberty is no vice. And let me remind you also that moderation in the defense of justice is no virtue."

These were the powerful and stirring words of an American patriot with sweeping vision and deep commitment to the ideals on which this nation was founded.

What he said from the gaudy lectern in the Cow Palace might have been the words of our revolutionary forebears, who rose up against kingly oppression and carved this new nation from the American wilderness. Surely they were "extremists" to the nth degree; so, too, was Patrick Henry when in 1775 he uttered the rousing words "Give me liberty or give me death." Other stalwart and impassioned defenders of freedom were similarly expressing their views, such as pamphleteer Tom Paine, who wrote near the end of the eighteenth century, "A thing moderately good is not so good as it ought to be. Moderation in temper is always a virtue; but moderation in principle is always a vice."

What John F. Kennedy said in his inaugural address in 1961, words quoted fondly to this day, promised "extreme" measures—"we shall pay any price, bear any burden, meet any hardship, support any friend, oppose any foe"—to assure the survival and success of liberty.

Washington Post editor Ben Bradlee said he felt Barry Goldwater's words on extremism would have been widely heralded by the media if they had been spoken by Kennedy.

And Martin Luther King Jr., from his jail cell in Birmingham only a year before Goldwater's nomination, asked, "Was not Jesus an extremist for love? Was not Paul an extremist for the Christian gospel? So the question is not whether we will be extremists, but what kind of extremists we will be."

Every nation or group of dissidents willing to take risks—even die—for freedom can be considered "extremist" in the best and most noble sense of that word. Barry Goldwater's words placed him in that genre of patriotism.

Those words brought roaring delegates to their feet in a gesture of acclamation on that July night in 1964. But a combination of anti-Goldwater forces used those very words to paint the cantankerous, unpredictable westerner as a scary extremist and assure his annihilation at the polls:

- There was the "liberal" wing of the Republican Party—Rockefeller, Scranton, Romney, Lodge, and yes, even Richard Nixon for the expedient moment, the so-called eastern establishment—fighting to retain their longtime control of the GOP, whose relentless attacks on Goldwater provided a virtual game plan to be used against him in the fall campaign.

- There was Goldwater's opponent, Lyndon B. Johnson, who became president after Kennedy's death. Johnson, crafty, ruthless, and power hungry, aimed for a record-setting plurality in November. His key aide, Bill Moyers, worked closely with Doyle Dane Bernbach, the New York ad agency, to craft the vicious and scary TV commercial depicting a little girl in a field incinerated by a nuclear blast.

• There was the mass media, a wolf pack on the attack, which vilified Goldwater mercilessly. It got so bad that John S. Knight, then publisher of the defunct *Chicago Daily News* and *Akron Beacon Journal*, and at the time a lion of journalism, wrote, "I can no longer stand silently by and watch the shabby treatment Goldwater is getting from most of the news media." He seared the press in several biting columns but changed few minds.

• There were the millions of ordinary voters, brainwashed to believe Goldwater was indeed a dangerous extremist with horns and forked tail, who, as president, would employ nuclear weapons and "dismantle" Social Security—both gross, but lethal, canards.

"Never once in all my statements or my writings on foreign policy had I ever advocated nuclear war as a solution to a troubled world," Goldwater said in a voice trembling with indignation. From the moderate wing, Eisenhower, elder statesman and balance wheel, stood above the pressure to support "anybody but Goldwater," wavered briefly, but maintained the neutrality he had promised.

But he, too, was greatly troubled by Goldwater's "extremism" quote and summoned the nominee to his Fairmont Hotel suite the next morning to explain the meaning behind his words, which many branded inflammatory. Ike told Barry he was worried by the widespread negative reaction all across the country. Goldwater was undaunted.

"When you landed your troops in Normandy," the senator reminded the old commander, "it was an exceedingly extreme action taken because you were committed to the defense of freedom."

There was a pause, according to Goldwater, and then "Ike's face broke into that inimitable grin. 'I guess you're right, Goldwater. I never thought of it that way.'"

My own feeling—as a lifelong history buff with a degree in American history—is that those stirring words deserve on merit to be included among the foremost utterances of American leaders over the more than two centuries of our existence as a free nation.

Goldwater always said, "Freedom is the single word that has expressed my political philosophy throughout my public life. The two simple declarative sentences [from Goldwater's acceptance speech in 1964] summed up my approach to the presidency. For I intended to do my utmost in the defense of liberty and to pursue justice in a manner far removed from the average."

Most political sound bites of recent years veer far from the admirable founding principles of this nation and instead make blatant pitches to greed, selfishness, prejudice, and self-interest.

Goldwater's "reminder" to the GOP delegates and the nation rose above that self-indulgent level and promised he would do all in his power to preserve and expand our precious liberty, and make that elusive "true" justice a high priority.

Many who read this book weren't even alive, or were infants or young children, when Barry Goldwater ran for president in 1964. Many more will recall little more than his name.

Yet, he was one of the resolute shapers of the history of the momentous twentieth century and the godfather of the conservative movement that has become dominant in today's America but that he felt had been distorted by far-out opportunists who have hijacked true conservatism's popularity for their own disparate ends.

The fateful words Barry Goldwater uttered on July 17, 1964, in San Francisco deserve to be preserved to define and highlight the singular character of this bastion of freedom. Only a few people are left on the American scene who come close to Barry Goldwater at a time this nation desperately needs more like him.

9

The People Were Cheated:
JFK Versus Barry
Was Not to Be

*Bill, I knew the minute I heard the news Jack Kennedy
was shot I had no chance to be president.*
— BG TO AUTHOR,
RUSSELL SENATE OFFICE
BUILDING, MARCH 1983

THE AMERICAN PEOPLE in 1964 were cheated out of a
classic presidential confrontation that surely would
have restored their faith in the tattered political
process.

It would have been a hard, honest, illuminating battle for the leadership of the free world between two
friendly antagonists with widely differing viewpoints
but a shared love for their country: President John

Fitzgerald Kennedy versus Senator Barry Morris Goldwater. Kennedy, the suave, affluent, Harvard-educated
easterner, and Goldwater, blunt, straight-talking product of the New West, godfather of twentieth-century
conservatism.

But it was not to be, as Kennedy was struck down in
Dallas, and Goldwater reluctantly faced in Lyndon B.
Johnson a "wheeler-dealer" he detested and mistrusted.

Few are aware of the genuinely warm, easy friendship between Jack Kennedy, then forty-six, and Barry
Goldwater, fifty-five, two thoroughly decent philosophical opposites in the prime of their political lives.

From the first stirrings of political movement on his
behalf, Goldwater had been a stubbornly reluctant candidate for president. At no time did Barry have that
insatiable obsession to run for president—to be president—that grips some politicians. His mission was
more one of selling his conservative philosophy, of
conveying to ordinary Americans the conservative
principles he felt would "save" his beloved country.

But as his reputation grew, both in the Senate and on
the speech circuit, especially as chairman of the Senate
Campaign Committee, which took him on a grueling
schedule from coast to coast, pressure mounted on

Goldwater to run. He was the unquestioned leader of that sizable segment of the Republican Party that represented a commitment to his brand of conservatism; he was the only effective challenger of the long-dominant eastern forces that controlled the GOP.

Camelot notwithstanding, President John F. Kennedy's early tenure had been troubled and controversial. The Bay of Pigs fiasco had made him appear wobbly and uncertain in confronting crisis. There was no assurance he could be reelected.

Jack and Barry were uncommonly good friends at opposite ends of the political spectrum. Even though they disagreed on the big issues, they took to each other warmly on a personal level. Their relationship in many respects was both improbable and remarkable.

In his 1979 autobiography, Goldwater recalled, "There were four relationships in Congress that meant a great deal to me—with the Kennedys, Senator Paul Laxalt, and two Arizona congressmen, [Democrat] Mo Udall and [Republican] John Rhodes."

Consider: only four among all the colleagues he knew and worked with over three decades in the Senate. Laxalt, a conservative Republican from Nevada who became the closest Senate confidant of President

Ronald Reagan, two home-state friends of long standing—and "the Kennedys," liberal Democrats, Jack and Bobby. He was closest to JFK. In retrospect, an amazing revelation by Goldwater of a genuinely improbable linkage.

"Jack Kennedy had come to the Senate at the same time I did," Barry said in his autobiography. "We were on opposite sides of the aisle, but I found him likable, aggressive, and consistent in his support of the liberal Democratic policies."

Barry explained his affection and fascination: "With the Kennedys, patriotism drew us together. Jack loved this country, and I believe all the Kennedy brothers' lives were affected by losing Joe [their oldest brother] in World War II. The Kennedys returned the compliment. Ted expressed their view to a friend of mine: 'I think my brother, Jack, liked Barry Goldwater so much because Barry was so good at poking fun at himself,'" a talent often attributed to JFK.

Ted continued, "I believe just about everybody in Washington likes Barry today because he came out of his 1964 loss with grace and humor. He started over."

Ultimately Goldwater became intrigued by the idea of running against Jack Kennedy. He thought the contrast would be striking and the campaign illuminating for the voting public.

"He was Hah-vahd; I was the New West," Barry told me in a 1994 interview. "He was the darling of the eastern establishment; I was the hard-nosed frontier conservative. He was suave and dashing; I was possibly a little gauche, more informal, less programmed, and more inclined to blurt out my views."

For that reason, Kennedy, believing Goldwater would be the Republican nominee, was confident he could "take" Barry in a good, close race. He assumed that the "shoot-from-the-lip" westerner would step into enough cowpatties and make enough verbal blunders to assure the president of easy reelection.

That JFK had high regard for Barry is evidenced by this comment in 1963, passed on by brother Ted: "I really like Barry," said Jack Kennedy. "And if he's the Republican nominee and I'm licked, at least it will be on the issues. At least the people will have a clear choice."

Goldwater likewise felt keenly they would run against each other by articulating plainly their differences on matters of great moment to the nation. It would have been an "uplifting campaign, a damn good race," Goldwater told me.

"Jack and I even talked about touring the country together and putting on a kind of Lincoln-Douglas debate. We were that close personally. We'd fly from town to town and spend a half hour or so in friendly, but deadly serious, combat."

Barry was convinced that such an issue-oriented give-and-take would have a positive impact and possibly even ignite apathetic voters, probably increase citizen turnout and involvement, and erase some of the prevailing cynicism about politics.

Despite his positive feelings for Jack Kennedy, and their friendship, Goldwater stressed in his autobiography that he had been "sharply critical of the Kennedy administration." He stated, "I opposed its domestic policies and called for a congressional investigation of the Bay of Pigs. Even so, my personal relations with the president were warm and friendly. He took it for granted I would be his opponent in 1964 and offered advice." The relationship of the two likely foes for the highest office in the land defied logic. It may have reflected the singular qualities of the two men.

Kennedy's advice to Goldwater: "Don't announce too soon, Barry. The minute you do, you will be the target. If you give them eighteen months to shoot you down, they will probably be able to do it." Contrast that attitude with the downright nasty political warfare of the 1990s.

"The president believed as I did that presidential campaigns should be centered on the substantive differences between policies advocated by contending candidates," said Goldwater. "He was offended by the injection of trivial matters, by the distortions that usually disfigure such contests. Kennedy thought that if we could engage in a serious dialogue—direct the voters' attention to the nation's major problems—and then offer alternative solutions, we would be making a constructive contribution to the public's understanding of the complexities of government.

"We talked seriously of campaigning together, appearing before the same audiences. He once reminded me of an article I had written on the general subject of how to be a good opponent, making five points:

"First of all, it is fine to oppose, but do not hate.

"Second, keep your sense of humor.

"Third, always oppose positively.

"Fourth, learn all the tricks of campaigning.

"Fifth, applaud your opponent if he is right."

Can you imagine any of the recent and current presidential adversaries behaving in that manner and giving sincere advice to each other?

Goldwater continued: "I knew the Kennedy campaign team would play for keeps. I was aware of the enormous advantage of incumbency. But Jack Kennedy and I had always been able to express our opinions to each other without rancor. I respected all his many fine qualities.

"He confessed there was merit in some of my proposals. We both believed the federal government was overgrown, unwieldy, almost unmanageable. Where I blamed the selfishness of certain labor leaders for some of our economic problems, the president said Big Business was at fault. He wanted a strong national defense capability and believed [Defense] Secretary [Robert] McNamara and his whiz kids at the Pentagon were providing it. I thought McNamara was deliberately and systematically reducing our defense posture in pursuit of parity with the Russians.

"Kennedy believed his general reduction in taxes would stimulate the economy. I thought it would lead to higher deficits and more inflation and would threaten bankruptcy. Kennedy was right on this. His tax cut did stimulate the economy. Federal tax collection increased even at the lower rate.

"To Jack Kennedy, politics was a kind of game, like touch football or a sailing contest. Winning was all that mattered. He had no deep-seated overriding political-philosophical convictions to constitute any insurmountable barrier between us. . . . While I saw the policies of the Democratic Party as threatening and destructive, and, therefore, to be violently opposed, he saw them as mechanisms, attractive political gimmicks, devised to achieve political victory. . . .

"We will never know whether a Kennedy-Goldwater contest would have been conducted on the lines we projected, but it presented an intriguing possibility. I was painfully aware that even under the best of conditions, I held the short end of the stick."

Barry Goldwater was plagued by indecision. He had no obsession to run. But he hoped that if he entered the race against his good friend, "Jack Kennedy would somehow keep his commitments. We would lift this presidential campaign above the petty, conniving scheming which had flawed every political race in my experience. We would present the American voters with an opportunity to make a reasoned decision based on contending political philosophies rather than on personality."

By any measure, this was an idealistic approach to what typically has been a somewhat tawdry process. If it had become a reality, it would have cleansed and lifted the process, and probably washed away some of the cynicism so prevalent and growing as the nation embarks on a new century.

During this period, Goldwater, goaded by core conservatives who saw him as their standard-bearer, edged closer to launching his campaign. He and Jack Kennedy even joked and needled each other about the prospect of a showdown between them. But it was not to be. Verging on tears, Goldwater told me of his feelings of disbelief and grief when he learned of his good friend's assassination in Dallas.

Some years later, Barry told me, "Bill, I knew the minute I heard the news Jack Kennedy was shot I had no chance to be president."

One unfortunate episode, a distressing but unintended error, clouded the relationship between Barry and another eminent American at that horrendous moment in history.

At almost the same time as Kennedy's benumbing demise, Barry's mother-in-law, Mrs. Ray Prescott Johnson, died in Phoenix. The senator halted his presidential campaign to fly the body of Peggy's mother to her home in Muncie, Indiana, for the funeral services.

A wire service report, apparently by the Associated Press, wrongly had Goldwater going to Indiana for a campaign event, and Walter Cronkite, the widely revered CBS anchorman, read the incoming tape and broadcast that version, which made Goldwater seem callous and disrespectful of the Kennedy tragedy, despite his closeness to Jack.

"I was never so angry in my life, and I phoned to say, 'Mr. Cronkite, I don't know you. I've always respected you. But you just told CBS viewers a blatant lie. I'm not here in Indiana to make a political speech, but to help bury my mother-in-law.'"

It was an honest mistake based on a report from a normally reliable source; Cronkite quickly apologized and retracted the erroneous report.

"I accepted Cronkite's apology and, to this day, hold no rancor against him. He's a personable and honorable man." Goldwater expressed to me his "enormous respect" for Cronkite, who came to be known as "the most trusted man in America" and continues as a towering presence in the realm of current affairs.

Cronkite took umbrage at Barry's Vesuvian eruption and "chewing out," feeling Goldwater should have known he wouldn't have done such a thing deliberately, but rather was the victim of an unfortunate error by a trusted source. Goldwater was on edge over media distortions all through his campaign, which caused him to overreact and lash out.

Cronkite still remembers the long-ago flap, but when I asked for his impressions of Goldwater, he recalled the senator positively with cool, detached approval.

The death of JFK dashed Barry's enthusiasm for the presidential race. He said to Peggy while in Muncie, "That does it. I'm definitely not going to run."

She was pleased, and "the faint glow of a smile crossed her face."

His overwhelming reason, Goldwater said, was his distaste for Lyndon Johnson.

"There had to be a line of battle where principles and beliefs clashed openly for the public to see." That's what Barry and Jack had envisioned. But there was no chance that this scenario would occur in a race against Johnson, the consummate "wheeler-dealer" and "unprincipled politician."

"I was convinced," said Barry, "that the American people were not ready for three presidents in little more than a year."

So, Goldwater, shaken by Jack Kennedy's death and "having no lust for the power of the office," was prepared to opt out. Now maybe Peggy finally would have Barry to herself for a while. But the senator at this point was not the master of his fate. Too many good friends and true believers were counting on him alone to carry the conservative torch. Only he could lead the movement, they told him.

On December 8, 1963, Goldwater met with a small cadre of backers he trusted most. They were quickly dubbed by the press the "Arizona Mafia," comprising mainly longtime friends and associates with precious little actual political experience, and none in national campaigns. Barry clearly felt more comfortable with cronies rather than with the more savvy leaders of the

Draft Goldwater movement, such as F. Clifton White, a college professor and astute political organizer; Congressman John Ashbrook of Ohio; and William A. Rusher, a Harvard-educated lawyer and compatriot of William F. Buckley Jr. in launching *National Review*. Goldwater said categorically, "The Draft Goldwater movement was responsible for my nomination."

True "drafts" in politics are largely nonexistent, mainly figments of the imagination of an obsessed candidate, who engineered the draft in his or her own behalf. But the Draft Goldwater movement was a genuine draft. Clif White was determined when he told Goldwater of their ambitious plans to get him nominated.

"I told him I knew I could not stop him," Barry said, "but I would not encourage him."

By the time of Barry's meeting in December of 1963, he had concluded that "no Republican could prevail against Lyndon Johnson." He opened the small session with these bleak words: "Our cause is lost."

But the men in the room thought otherwise; they had, Barry said, "a substantial investment in a Goldwater candidacy."

These men, clearly without national campaign know-how, "would become the heart and muscle of the Goldwater election team." There was Bill Baroody, a public policy expert whose experience was intellectual and theoretical; Barry's longtime friend Denison Kitchel, who became campaign chairman; speechwriter Karl Hess, who turned radical left after Goldwater's defeat; Jay Hall, friend and political thinker; Dean Burch, a Goldwater intimate whom Barry would install as GOP national chairman; Arizona congressman John Rhodes; and three conservative U.S. senators, Carl Curtis of Nebraska, William Knowland of California, and Norris Cotton of New Hampshire.

"Cotton's words endeared him to me," Goldwater said in his autobiography. "Circumstances had made me the leader. I could not in good conscience refuse the responsibility, no matter how distasteful the prospect, no matter how uncertain the outcome. . . . He said it was my duty to lead the conservative forces. He did not predict victory. He reminded me there was more to life than winning.

"I had planted the flag on the hilltop; now I must defend that flag."

Goldwater named the late Richard Kleindienst, a Harvard Law graduate, one-term Arizona legislator, and head of Governor Paul Fannin's campaign for a second term, as director of the Goldwater for President Committee. Dick Kleindienst was the most seasoned of the initial squad and later had a major role in the Nixon presidential campaign of 1968.

This, then, was the somewhat green team on which Goldwater would rely to overcome huge odds in the battle that lay ahead.

10

The Senate as Goldwater's Bully Pulpit

We are all required to pay rent for the space
we occupy on this earth . . . the good Lord had been
most gracious to us, and perhaps by helping to preserve
our freedoms, I could make a real contribution
[as a U.S. Senator].
—BG, *WITH NO APOLOGIES*, 1951

BARRY GOLDWATER loved the Senate—and had "many friends on both sides of the aisle," said colleague Bob Dole—but, predictably, he found its tedious rituals and Byzantine maneuvering downright boring and often pointless. He was more of an action-oriented doer than a legislative dawdler; he simply didn't have the patience to tolerate the Senate's tortoiselike pace and deliberate ways. What the Senate gave him was the bully pulpit to sell his vision of what would "save" his beloved America, and he participated more at the fringes of the Upper House than at its core.

Goldwater, in fact, was content to let a fellow senator such as Democrat Robert Byrd, the at-times overbearing, somewhat theatrical, clout-heavy craftsman from West Virginia, carry the intricate legislative burdens.

Goldwater was more caught up in a few grander themes, such as those that expanded personal liberty or choked off reckless pork-barrel spending at taxpayer expense or kept the labor bosses somewhat in check. At no time did he consider his Senate career to be his proudest achievement.

This is in no way an attempt to summarize Goldwater's thirty-year Senate tenure, but rather to cite what Barry considered his most meaningful Senate accomplishment, as well as his head-to-head Senate involvement with two presidents.

Even though Goldwater credited the coattails of triumphant Dwight D. Eisenhower for his unexpected 1952 upset win in his first Senate race in the Democratic stronghold of Arizona, and Ike held the young firebrand in generally high regard, the two tangled on occasion.

"It was impossible not to like Dwight David Eisenhower," said Goldwater. "There was no pretense about Ike. That wonderfully infectious grin could totally disarm his critics. He and Mamie were as American as apple pie. His career validated the American Dream."

Early on, Goldwater openly expressed his disappointment over some of Ike's actions—or inaction—as president. "In matters political," Goldwater said, "I found Ike to be extremely naive. He was a product of the military."

Four months after Barry took his Senate seat, he broke a long-standing informal rule that freshmen should "be seen but not heard." He spoke out against granting standby authority to the president to impose wage and price controls. Ike responded with a two-word pat on the back: "Atta boy."

Early in Ike's second term, Goldwater broke ranks. He was increasingly distressed that Eisenhower was exhibiting some of the same "fiscal irresponsibility which had so long been the sole property of the Democratic administrations." In a Senate speech, he apologized for taking on the president, then spoke bluntly: "A $71.8 billion budget not only shocks me, it weakens my faith in the constant assurances we have received from this administration that its aim was to cut spending, balance the budget, reduce debt, cut taxes—in short, live within our means. It is disillusioning to see the Republican Party plunging headlong into the same dismal state experienced by the liberal Democrats." Goldwater reminded Ike what he'd said in 1952: "We must eliminate deficits and waste, cut crazy spending programs."

"I didn't personally blame Ike," Barry said in his autobiography. "I knew that many of the modern liberal Republicans close to him believed the administration must turn left to regain public approval. . . . I was greatly reassured when I discovered that Ike had not taken offense at my remarks. In private he almost agreed with me. I had planted my flag. I had no regrets."

But the most direct break came on legislation backed by Ike to curb some of the rawer practices of Big Labor, which fell short of its intent. After an uncomfortable rift, Barry made his point and his peace, and the air was cleared, with Goldwater carrying the day resoundingly.

After a two-year investigation into corrupt labor practices, debate began on Senate Bill 1555, the so-called (John) Kennedy–(Sam) Ervin Bill.

Barry said, "The measure was represented as an effective labor law reform. It wasn't. I offered some eighteen amendments, all of which were turned down. . . . The bill, as now developed by this body, in terms of the conditions it professes to cure, is like a flea bite to a bull elephant."

The president was on record as favoring labor law reform. When the bill came up for a vote, Goldwater voted against it and then left for a speaking date in Philadelphia. By radio, he picked up the results of the vote: 90 for, 1 against. Barry was the only senator to vote "nay."

Early the next Monday, Barry was summoned to the White House. Ike was hot. The president "wanted to know why the hell I had voted against a bill which was badly needed. . . . He asked sarcastically if I thought everyone in the Senate was out of step but me."

Barry responded, "Mr. President, this bill is a sham and a farce. Have you read it?"

Ike came back testily that he didn't have time to read every bill that passed the Congress. He said his staff told him it was a good measure that would do the job, and "apparently ninety members of the United States Senate thought so, too."

"I told him either he had been deliberately deceived or else his staffers were too damn dumb to understand the English language." Ike's face reddened, and it was clear to Barry that his volcanic temper, which showed only occasionally and in short bursts, was about to erupt. "I knew I was in trouble."

Before the president could say anything more, Goldwater spoke up: "Please listen to me for just a minute. This bill won't prevent blackmail picketing, and let me tell you just what that is. A union representative comes to management with a proposed union contract. He issues an ultimatum—sign or be picketed. The owner refuses because his employees don't want to join the union. A picket line is set up manned by professional pickets who are not employees of the company. Deliveries are cut off, customers intimidated. That's blackmail picketing, Mr. President.

"This bill doesn't prevent secondary boycott, and let me tell you what that is. The employees of a company decide not to join a union. Instead of picketing the company's plant, unions picket the stores which sell the product.

"The bill ignores the right of union members to have a voice in the affairs of the union's operations. It won't prevent union bosses from looting union treasuries. It's a bad bill, Mr. President, and that's why I voted against it. Ike grinned. 'Thank you, Barry,' he said. 'You've given me a lot to think about, and I'm going to think about it.'"

True to his word, Eisenhower ordered a new team from his staff to conduct a fresh study of the bill that Barry opposed so vehemently. Exactly 101 days later, President Eisenhower went on national TV to detail the deficiencies of the Kennedy-Ervin Bill. He urged Congress instead to pass an "effective labor reform bill."

Less than a month later, the Senate reversed itself by a vote of 95 to 2. "Kennedy-Ervin was scuttled," said Goldwater, "and Landrum-Griffin passed. I gave Ike the credit for that turnaround and tried to thank him for it, but at the time he was very unhappy with me because I had made a Senate speech calling his budget 'a dime-store New Deal.'" Small wonder Eisenhower was piqued.

While Ike seemed to be fond of Barry, he also found him exasperating on such occasions. Once at Gettysburg, Ike welcomed Goldwater but also let him have it: "Barry, you speak too quick and too loud."

On another occasion, Goldwater was asked by a reporter about Ike's brother, Milton, as a possible candidate for president. Milton was more liberal than Ike and, in Barry's mind, a kind of pointy-headed academic type. So he blurted out, "One Eisenhower is enough," which could be read as disrespectful of Ike, who was suitably miffed. Goldwater apologized.

In spite of such misunderstandings and gaffes, Eisenhower was a hero to Goldwater, who summed up his feelings this way: "Ike's belief in the virtue of the American Republic never wavered. He believed in the goodness of the American people and trusted them. He devoted all his energy and all his talents to the preservation of the American Republic. It was a blessed privilege to know him and to serve with him this country we both have loved so long and so well."

Ronald Reagan's path to the presidency was paved by his role as an eloquent television advocate for Goldwater in the 1964 campaign, enunciating Barry's conservative platform with his engaging oratorical skills. He became the beneficiary of Goldwater's stunning conservative breakthrough despite the Arizonan's overwhelming defeat.

But the two good friends had reservations about each other, and Goldwater did not hesitate to put down the former GE pitchman and to speak out when he felt Reagan erred in the presidency. "He's just an actor," said Goldwater when asked to comment for a commemorative film on Reagan in 1987. When Barry first met Reagan, "he was about as far to the left as you can get. . . . He was never what I would call a complete conservative." That was when Reagan was head of a Hollywood union for the film fraternity. Once when Goldwater and actor George Murphy visited Reagan at his home, Reagan called them a "couple of Fascist bastards." Despite Reagan's portrayal of himself as a "budget-buster," Goldwater criticized him for not cutting back on spending, not stopping welfare, not reducing the bureaucracy. "Had I been in Reagan's place," he often said in his later years, "this country would never have gone $3 trillion in debt."

The most notable breach occurred when Goldwater, who became chairman of the Senate Select Committee on Intelligence in 1981 after Reagan's election, concluded he had been lied to by William Casey, Reagan's choice to head the Central Intelligence Agency (CIA). On the Senate floor, Senator Joseph Biden, Democrat from Delaware, in 1984 said the CIA had been directly involved in mining three harbors on both the Atlantic and Pacific coasts of Nicaragua. Goldwater replied that he had no knowledge of such CIA activity and therefore did not believe it to be true.

When Goldwater learned that the CIA had in fact mined the harbors on Reagan's orders, he was furious. He felt betrayed because the president had vowed to keep his committee fully informed about "significant" covert actions. This was surely "significant."

"Such mining," thundered Goldwater, "was tantamount to an act of war. International law is very clear on the point. Nicaragua is a coastal nation dependent on its harbors for food and other necessities. . . ."

Goldwater promptly wrote Casey: "All this past weekend, I've been trying to figure out how I can most easily tell you of my feelings about the discovery of the president having approved mining. . . . It gets down to one little, simple phrase: I am pissed off! . . . Bill, this is no way to run a railroad, and I find myself in a hell of a quandary. I am forced to apologize to members of the Intelligence Committee because I did not know the facts on this. At the same time, my counterpart in the House did know.

"The president has asked us to back his foreign policy. Bill, how can we back his foreign policy when we don't know what the hell he is doing? Lebanon, yes, we all knew he sent troops over there. But mine the harbors in Nicaragua? This is an act violating international law. It is an act of war. For the life of me, I don't see how we are going to explain it. . . .

"I don't like this. I don't like it one bit from the president or from you. . . . The deed has been done, and in the future, if anything like this happens, I am going to raise one hell of a lot of fuss about it in public."

Casey lied in defending himself, according to Goldwater, saying, "The agency (CIA) has not only complied with the letter of the law in our briefings, but with the spirit of the law as well."

"I really was steaming about Casey's disregard for the facts," Goldwater said. Then, Robert MacFarlane, the president's assistant for national security affairs, "bombed me" in a widely quoted speech at the U.S. Naval Academy. He said that "every important detail" of the mining had been "shared in full with the proper oversight committees." Goldwater had flown off to Taiwan, but MacFarlane's words infuriated Senator Daniel Patrick Moynihan, Democratic vice chair of the Intelligence Committee. Said Pat Moynihan, "Sonofabitch, he's calling Barry Goldwater a liar. It's not true. . . . I'm not going to let this stand."

So, Moynihan went to David Brinkley of ABC and, "putting up his political dukes" on TV, boomed that he would have no choice but to resign unless Casey and MacFarlane retracted their statements. Goldwater called it a "bravissimo performance." Both backed off, MacFarlane blaming Casey for misleading him.

On Iran-Contra, in which Reagan and Casey went around Congress and turned to Admiral William Poindexter and Oliver North to do their bidding, Goldwater believes the clandestine maneuvers "didn't accomplish a damn thing except to harm Reagan's presidency. . . . I believe the president did know of the diversion of Iranian funds to the Contras. If he knew about the sale of weapons to an enemy country and various ways in which Americans were aiding the Contras, Reagan knew about the transfer of funds. He had to know. The White House explanation makes him out either to be a liar or incompetent. . . . Unfortunately, I believe that the Iran-Contra crisis cost Ronald Reagan the chance to be among the greatest presidents of this century. History will judge him much more harshly because of that unfortunate episode. The selling of arms to terrorist Iran unquestionably did the president irreparable harm. He will never regain his former stature. Now I think history will give him a passing grade—in some instances, such as domestic policy, an outstanding mark—but not the credit he deserves overall."

In 1985, during his fifth and final term, at age seventy-six and hurting, this fierce patriot, putting country ahead of all else, dug in for a battle that might have been the toughest and most painful—except, of course, for his presidential foray—of his long, honorable career of public service. He was determined to "fix the system" that he knew "was broke and needed fixing." That would be America's bloated, inefficient military establishment, which he believed had deteriorated to the point where it threatened the country's ability to win a major war.

Then chairman of the Senate Armed Services Committee, Goldwater proposed a far-reaching, radical overhaul of the entrenched Pentagon bureaucracy, an initiative treated as heresy by the top brass of the three service branches and their potent civilian and congressional champions. His main ally was Georgia Democrat Sam Nunn, ranking minority member of the committee and Goldwater's good friend.

Of Nunn, Goldwater said, "With Sam, I'd take on the devil in hell." Goldwater shocked Bob Dole when he told him he might support Nunn for president.

It often seemed, as they pressed their initiative, that Goldwater and Nunn were taking on the entire U.S. military establishment, the world's mightiest, at the height of their battle for a reformed Pentagon. Barry characterized the angry and ruffled opposition's reaction as "something like the onset of World War III."

Goldwater was a dyed-in-the-wool hawk, a military aficionado throughout his public career (brother Bob told me, "Barry always loved and was intrigued by the military") and a consistent supporter of a powerful defense arsenal, which made his sweeping reform proposal all the more surprising, but which also made him the ideal public figure to undertake such a controversial, even radical, mission.

Barry knew far better than most the Machiavellian ways of the sprawling military bureaucracy, the stormy rivalry among the frightfully independent service branches, the big-dollar waste and inefficiency and extravagance fueled in large part by the military contractors and suppliers.

He was acutely aware of President Eisenhower's warning as he left office against "the grave implications of an immense military establishment and a large arms industry" and his declaration that "we must guard against the acquisition of unwarranted influence . . . by the military-industrial complex. The potential for the disastrous rise of misplaced power exists and will persist." This from the military hero of World War II after two terms as the nation's chief executive. It was a somber, far-seeing warning that Barry took seriously.

"The politics of the military makes Republicans and Democrats seem like Boy Scouts," Goldwater stated disappointedly. "The chief concern of the top military brass, the Joint Chiefs of Staff, was their turf—power." They were fully prepared to launch all-out war—against Goldwater, Nunn, and other reformers for the sole purpose of defending their power and perquisites.

But Goldwater was powerfully motivated by his view of the pressing need to reform the U.S. defense organization and command system, "which was clearly flawed and dangerous for everyone." Nunn was equally convinced. Goldwater had witnessed, with ever deep-

ening concern, the disaster of Pearl Harbor, and other
blunders on a lesser scale, such as the muddled invasion
of Grenada ("a minefield of errors"), the badly botched
Iran hostage rescue mission, and the terrorist killing
of Marines in Lebanon.

Goldwater attributed these "fiascos" in significant
part to a divided command and resulting poor communication and cooperation among the services. This
must be corrected, he argued, before it costs still more
lives, the result of military foul-ups and lack of coordinated effort. He feared the deadly potential for further calamity, even defeat, and the massive loss of
young lives if the United States should be drawn into a
major war under the then-existing organization and
command structure of our armed forces.

In concert with Nunn and other allies in the Senate,
Goldwater determined to take bold, unprecedented
action. While they knew the resistance would be sharp
and stiff, neither anticipated the scope and intensity of
the opposition. They found themselves taking on the
irate mother grizzly protecting her cubs, the savage
military beast defending its traditional prerogatives.

"None of us," said Goldwater, "expected the emotion, particularly the open bitterness, expressed by the

Joint Chiefs and their congressional allies. . . . When Nunn and I began to make our move, I wouldn't have bet more than a sawbuck on our chances of success."

The extent of the opposition mounted by the military brass and their avid supporters is instructive and at least somewhat frightening.

On February 3, 1986, at 6 P.M., a historic meeting was convened in the Tank, a big, barren, top-security meeting room in the Pentagon. "The subject," said Goldwater, "was a legislative proposal that would launch the most sweeping reorganization of U.S. military leadership in three decades."

The "host" was Admiral William J. Crowe Jr., the deceptively smart, bulky chairman of the Joint Chiefs of Staff. Goldwater had told Crowe earlier that no others from his Armed Services Committee, except Nunn and several staff members, were invited to the session, even though three Republican senators, John Warner of Virginia, Jeremiah Denton of Alabama, and Phil Gramm of Texas, all strong opponents of reorganization, had sought to attend.

The Tank "came to life," Goldwater said, when the top military brass—silver stars on their epaulets, gold braid glinting on their sleeves, rows of gaudy ribbons emblazoning their immaculate uniforms—arrived. The four service chiefs, members of the Joint Chiefs of Staff, and four staff officers sat across the table. The chiefs were General Charles A. Gabriel of the Air Force, General John A. Wickham Jr. of the Army, Admiral James D. Watkins, chief of Naval Operations, and General P. X. Kelley, Marine commandant. All were fervently opposed to the reorganization proposal, but their faces were uniformly impassive as the session began.

Goldwater had this explanation: "For decades, the JCS have been unwilling to present anything less than a united front to civilian authority. Nearly every JCS action has been unanimous. Interservice jealousies, mostly over funding and the scope of their military missions, have caused each branch to protect its own flanks. It became painfully evident that the services' first loyalty was to themselves. Unanimity was therefore forged only by compromises to which each service could agree. This resulted in delayed, compromised counsel to the president, defense secretary, and others. Tough issues were avoided. Clear, forceful solutions were, for the most part, doomed. The system was actually a disservice to the country and the services themselves."

Goldwater said Crowe's tack was to take aim at civilian authority's invasion of the chiefs' turf. Gabriel joined Crowe. The other three "launched a direct frontal attack on the bill.

"Wickham argued that the measure would destroy the independent judgment and professional integrity of the JCS by placing each chief under the civilian secretary of each department. Watkins and Kelley expanded on this theme in very emotional terms. Nunn and I were prepared for opposition but not this rancor.

"I tried to restore calm. I reminded the chiefs of my long efforts to strengthen the military. . . . I tried to tell them that a confrontational approach would not work with us. My conciliatory remarks had no impact. None at all. The chiefs, pressing a united front, intensified their attack. . . . They made no mention of their organization and command system, which was clearly flawed and dangerous for everyone.

"The crux of our plan was still on the table, and the chiefs had not said a word about it. Our central aim was to have U.S. sea, air, and ground forces fight as a team through a series of organizational and command changes within the services. These changes were crucial. . . ."

The JCS raised nine separate issues. Nunn and Goldwater had answers for each. "But the chiefs' message was clear: They didn't believe in reorganization, and they were telling us to go to hell." When they left, several would not even shake hands with Goldwater and Nunn.

"We quickly agreed that effective cooperation with the chiefs was now out of the question. None of us had expected the emotion, particularly the open bitterness. . . . Nor had we expected the discussion to frame itself around the simple issue of turf. . . . The staff turned to us for instructions on our first Senate markup meeting—spelling out precise provisions and language in the bill—scheduled for nine o'clock the following morning. Sam and I looked at each other. Our answer was clear and certain: Proceed as planned.

"The next morning, highly critical letters arrived from each service chief, as well as the civilian secretaries of the Army, Navy, and Air Force. Letters from Defense Secretary Caspar Weinberger and Chairman Crowe opposed our plan but were constructive.

"The battle was now out in the open. It was obvious that the entire might of the services and their allies in

Congress would be spent in defeating our plan." Goldwater said that, by his count, the Senate committee was split down the middle.

Powerful, noisy, all-out opposition came from Senator Warner, a former secretary of the Navy, and from John Lehman, who then held that post and "did everything he could to torpedo the plan." Historically, Congress has been a foe of centralized leadership of the military. Individual congressmen liked cozy links with the military so they could lobby cronies for lucrative military bases and supply contracts for their states and districts.

Despite long odds, Goldwater and Nunn had some things going for them. For one, President Eisenhower in 1958 had declared there was a greater need for more effective coordination of our armed forces: "We must free ourselves of emotional attachments to service systems of an era that is no more." His statement sent shock waves through the Pentagon, said Goldwater, but the JCS simply stalled, figuring Ike would soon be gone.

Then, as the bill was being studied in 1982, a statement by then-incumbent JCS chairman Marine General David Jones shook up the Pentagon bureaucracy with a pointed 6,500-word critique. Attempts to block Jones from issuing the statement failed. Four months before his retirement, Jones had "kicked ass," in the vernacular of the military. His remarks were pigeon-holed in the Pentagon archives until Goldwater and others "dusted them off."

This is some of what he said: "By law, if we (JCS) cannot reach unanimous agreement on an issue, we must inform the secretary of defense. We are under-standably reluctant to forward disagreements, so we invest much time and effort trying to accommodate differing views of the chiefs. . . . We need to spend more time on our war-fighting capabilities and less on an intramural scramble for resources." In effect, said Goldwater in summarizing, "Jones declared that the military should abolish its current system in which each service has a veto on virtually every stage of a routine staffing process. In other words, dump command by committee."

A similar attack on the existing system came from General Edward C. Meyer, Army chief of staff still on active duty.

The reformers were moving, and they introduced their defense reorganization measure in January 1985, when Goldwater was appointed chair of the Senate Armed Services Committee and Reagan started his second term as president.

The Pentagon forces and civilian opponents were adamant. "No way," they said, in unison.

Said Goldwater, "Lehman came out smoking. He fired off blistering letters to me and the others involved. The secretary described our proposal as "whiz-kid theories" that would make his post "ceremonial" and make a hash of our defense structure. . . . He dangled political plums at Congress, proposing to expand Navy home ports, which would mean jobs and federal largesse to favored districts.

"I, too, would play hardball. I put the defense budget, including all military promotions, on hold. I told them that just about everything connected with the military would be halted until we voted on reorganization."

That didn't stop the fired-up Lehman, but it resulted in a droll sidelight. His mother, a Goldwater backer in 1964 and later, objected to her son's plans. She wrote him, "Dear John: I don't know what the dispute is, but you're wrong."

Goldwater summarized what would be accomplished: "Our bill stressed, in accord with constitutional principles," the civilian supremacy of the president as commander in chief. It spelled out the role of the secretary of defense:

> The secretary has sole and ultimate power within the Department of Defense on any matter on which the secretary chooses to act. It greatly strengthened the JCS chairman in setting policies, drafting military strategies, and shaping Pentagon budgets. Many functions were removed from the four independent services and reassigned to the chairman alone. . . . The realignment created, in effect, a powerful partnership between the chairman and the secretary. . . . Field commanders would have much greater control over resources to accomplish their missions with far less direction in the hands of service bureaucrats in Washington. They would also have much greater control over their men. . . . For too long, our generals in the field have been without armies and our admirals without fleets. . . . The ad hoc plan developed for Iran and the mismatched planning affecting the Grenada invasion would be eliminated. . . . Policy assumptions and

military operational planning would no longer be disconnected, as they were for the Marines in Beirut. . . . More than ever before, the commanders in chief in the field will decide how to carry the war to the enemy. Our separate ground, sea, and air warfare by individual services is gone forever.

"It is now time," said Goldwater with his special eloquence, "for the brass to get off their ass." Even though the number of service personnel was reduced from 12 million to 2 million after the end of World War II, Goldwater pointed out, we had nearly the same number of high-ranking officers—almost 15,500 men and women. There were around 120 three-star generals and admirals—more than in 1945! As Sam Nunn put it dryly, "Apparently, it takes more admirals and generals to wage peace than to run a war."

The need for the reorganization was pressing and obvious. Congress spoke with a rare clarion voice: the National Defense Authorization Act of 1987 passed by 95 to 0 in the Senate and 406 to 4 in the House. The near unanimity was unprecedented on such a controversial measure, a tribute to the bulldog determination of Barry Goldwater, with the unstinting support of Sam Nunn.

Goldwater, in the twilight of his career, was elated as he neared the end of his fifth term.

"It's the only goddamn thing I've done in the Senate that's worth a damn. I can go home happy, sit on my hill, and shoot jackrabbits."

These three instances of Goldwater's most intense involvement in the Senate are only a selective recounting from his thirty-year Senate career. Barry did indeed love the Senate, not so much for itself, as a somewhat ponderous and at times stilted institution, but more for the camaraderie with good friends and colleagues, and for the bully pulpit it provided. By the end, he was in constant pain from a host of operations, including heart bypass and hip, knee, and shoulder replacement surgery, and all he really wanted was to go home to his beloved Arizona.

11

What if Barry Goldwater Had Won the Presidency?

Goldwater was the greatest president we never had.
—DAVID NOLAN,
LIBERTARIAN PARTY NEWS,
JULY 1998

- What if history were rewritten and President John F. Kennedy's life had been spared that dreadful day in Dallas?

- What if JFK and Barry Goldwater had opposed each other in the election of 1964 and civilly debated the issues in a latter-day reprise of the Lincoln-Douglas debates?

- What if Goldwater—unthinkable as it may seem—had won and ascended to the White House?

GOLDWATER HIMSELF would not speculate on what might have been if the two good friends had faced each other on the campaign trail. Looking back thirty-five years, I labor under no such restraints after Goldwater's annihilation at the hands of Lyndon Johnson by a landslide margin of 43 million votes to 27 million.

Those brought up on the legend of Camelot may find it inconceivable that the young prince wouldn't have soared on gossamer wings to a second term as president and on to mythic immortality. Much of the media, then and now, would find preposterous the notion that Barry Goldwater might even remotely have had a chance to upset JFK and become president.

Improbable? Of course. Impossible? Definitely not.

That scenario is by no means as far-fetched as it may seem. Kennedy was in trouble—despite the media-fueled hype and glitter that enveloped him—and his first term had not been a resounding, unalloyed success.

In November 1963, pollster Samuel Lubell predicted "a close election, with only a small edge in his [Kennedy's] favor" a full year before the election.

Senator John Tower, Texas Republican, offered his view that there was "a little too much Camelot going on . . . and it was rubbing a lot of people the wrong way."

If Kennedy had lived to run, it seems likely the election could have gone either way, with Kennedy holding the inevitable "edge" of incumbency.

Goldwater, facing insurmountable odds against LBJ in the aftermath of Kennedy's death, nonetheless pulled 27 million votes—a hard core unbudged by the anti-Goldwater vitriol spewed forth from the Johnson camp, Barry's Republican rivals, and the media attack cadre. Against Kennedy, on a more level playing field, following a cleaner, more enlightening, but no less hard-fought, issue-oriented campaign, Goldwater might well have polled the roughly 8.5 to 9 million more votes needed to give him a small popular majority.

While the media, liberally inclined, would have tilted to Kennedy, the two combatants were close enough personally to preclude the sort of vicious, gutter-level campaign that Johnson waged. The moderation of the candidates themselves probably would have tempered the media approach to some extent. JFK knew Goldwater was not a nuclear madman or "extremist." It would have been a tough, all-out encounter; the Kennedys always mean to win. JFK doubtless would have stressed his "cool" versus Barry's "hot," and Goldwater would have hammered at Kennedy's "failure of nerve" on the Bay of Pigs. But neither would have sought to destroy the other or to make fear of foe the overriding issue.

Scoff if you will, but what if Goldwater, godfather of a new conservatism with growing appeal, had amassed the electoral votes to win?

What kind of president would Goldwater have turned out to be?

By my measure, very good—one man's opinion as a Goldwater friend and admirer, a lifelong student of history and the presidency, with a degree in American history and civilization. Goldwater surely would have ranked in the top quarter of all our presidents, possibly higher. He would probably place among the top four or five in integrity and character. And near the top, with Harry Truman and Teddy Roosevelt, in decisiveness.

The people would have seen him, as he grew in the job, as he mellowed and matured, as earthy, direct, and truthful, admittedly displaying little of the drama and flair provided by Franklin D. Roosevelt. People would have been drawn to his plainspoken, no-nonsense demeanor, by a certain quality of populism, by his person-to-person, down-to-earth sincerity.

With President Goldwater, there would be no Nixon-style enemies list, wiretapping, and break-ins, none of the paranoia and siege mentality that marked Nixon's and some other presidencies.

There would be a fierce, uncommon devotion to freedom, the touchstone of Goldwater's entire political career. There would be no barging into bedrooms, no moral dictates, no strictures on private, personal decisions, but a high level of respect for the right of citizens to do as they chose within the law.

A hawk throughout his career, he would insist on a strong military but would knock heads when called for to keep the Pentagon egos in line. It was Goldwater, after all, who in his final Senate term led the titanic battle—"something like World War III," he said—for broad-based military reform, which he considered the high point of his thirty-year legislative career.

He described himself as something of a "skinflint" and said flatly that Reagan's cumulative $3 trillion

deficit couldn't have happened in a Goldwater administration. He would do what was necessary to shore up
Social Security and Medicare for the long haul, and he
would keep tight rein on the annual budget, something
promised by presidents but achieved only rarely.

He would be an environmental champion, goaded
in part by his love for the natural wonders of the U.S.
West. While many of his Republican colleagues were
"soft" on preserving the environment, Goldwater was
a staunch defender. In 1996, at age eighty-seven, he
enthusiastically became an honorary member of REP—
Republicans for Environmental Protection—a feisty
grassroots group at odds with GOP leadership that
has mushroomed across the nation. REP was launched
several years ago at the kitchen table of Martha Marks,
an elected member of the county board in Lake
County, Illinois, north of Chicago, who has been a tire-
less environmental advocate and turned down opportunities for political advancement to pursue her special
mission. In a letter to REP accepting honorary mem-
bership, Goldwater wrote, "I feel very strongly about
our beautiful deserts and want them to be there for
people to enjoy for many years, but I cannot assume a
lot of work on this project."

I'm convinced President Goldwater would have been an exemplary role model, a straight arrow setting a positive example for young and old alike. The personal moral tone in the White House would have risen sharply over that set during the presidencies of Clinton and Kennedy, and the media would have been deprived of the standard quota of scandals. Goldwater would blow his stack from time to time when the situation warranted, in the manner of Harry Truman, his prime role model. And he doubtless contributed to that volatility in his successor, Senator John McCain, who has shown some of the same maverick instincts as those of his elder hero from Arizona. That periodic stack-blowing, incidentally, is often the mark of a passionate believer rather than a political or boardroom conniver and status quo preserver.

Goldwater as president would have disappointed some hard-line conservatives, his onetime fans, just as he did during and after his senatorial career. They "just plain don't understand the meaning of the word *conservative*," he often said. The key words, which got him branded as a hot-eyed extremist during his acceptance speech in 1964, were *liberty* and *justice*, hallmarks of the American experiment in self-government and the foundation of his own deep-dyed political philosophy. If he was an "extremist" for liberty and justice, so be it.

He would have been, surprisingly to many but not to those who knew him, a strong proponent of equal rights and opportunity for minorities, including African Americans, Hispanics, and the Native Americans who were his Arizona friends and devoted backers. He would have advanced the cause of women and insisted on equal treatment for them.

Barry Goldwater realized that as a senator, he was the people's servant, and that attitude would follow him into the presidency. There would be little of the personal puffery and ego massaging so common among presidents. Goldwater did not even have a full-time public relations person in his 1964 campaign for the presidential nomination.

Who would have been his most vigorous foes? Not surprisingly, Big Labor. And the liberal establishment. Equally, in my view, and much more unexpectedly, Big Business, the Fortune 500, the huge financial conglomerates. Goldwater as president would be a foe of too-bigness, a trustbuster, somewhat akin to Teddy Roosevelt. In any showdown, he would be more inclined toward small and midsize entrepreneurial business than to the corporate goliaths, the Wall Street titans. He came, after all, from a modest family store that grew to prominence, and thus he understood the perils, pitfalls, and problems of the small enterprise struggling against much larger, better-financed behemoths.

His approach to the crime plague would be rational. He stated that there are too many people in prison who don't belong there and could be punished in other, less costly and confining ways. He wisely counseled against excessive grants of immunity, making the point that immunity often is an inducement to lie and thus to thwart the objective of justice. "I have always put very little faith," he said, "in the statement or claim of an individual who in return for talking about someone else gains immunity from prosecution." And he believed strongly that family solidarity, especially the involvement of mothers, is the best answer to juvenile crime and delinquency. He would almost certainly have urged the strict enforcement of laws on the books.

While he was characterized as cold and unfeeling in his 1964 campaign, that was yet another distortion. He made clear to me his intention to help those unable to cope and help themselves—people who are very young and very old, mentally ill, infirm, or undereducated—through a combination of private and public resources.

He opposed U.S. military incursions into trouble spots around the world except to support and defend U.S. interests. He believed in firmness in our dealings with other nations. He favored the Clinton policy in dealing with China and wanted to stimulate trade on a fair basis with foreign nations. Essentially, he was an internationalist intent on protecting U.S. interests as a foremost goal and stimulating exports of U.S. goods.

Goldwater was a foe of all forms of discrimination, and despite his opposition to the Civil Rights Act of 1964 on clearly defined constitutional grounds, this was his strong personal commitment. His lifelong actions and leadership in fighting and ending discrimination went far beyond typical, often hypocritical political rhetoric. In 1946, he provided for the first desegregated unit during the organization of the Arizona Air National Guard. That was two decades before the 1964 Civil Rights Bill. He was a longtime supporter of both the NAACP and the Urban League in Phoenix. And he insisted on desegregating the Goldwater's stores soon after he went to work there in his early twenties. "Never in my life," he said with passion, "had I ever advocated, suggested, or implied any form of racism." As president, he would have adhered strictly to his abhorrence of racism.

His overriding priority was the defense of freedom, of individual liberty, which he considered to be our most precious right.

President Goldwater would be honest, direct, a good communicator without the actor's embellishment of Reagan or the smooth, polished rhetoric of Clinton. His style would be unadorned and in the vernacular of the common man.

My guess is that he would have been reelected easily to a second term with at least 55 to 58 percent of the vote and would be looked upon widely as a people's president, a representative of common folk.

Our great presidents, by popular consensus, have had their stature expanded by their role as national leaders in wartime or national crisis: Washington, Lincoln, FDR, Truman, Eisenhower.

Of the peacetime presidents, Goldwater would in my view have stood comfortably in the front rank. His style might have come closest to that of Ike, whom he revered but frequently challenged from the Senate, and Truman, whose feisty, decisive ways he greatly admired. Political science professor Larry Sabato of the University of Virginia, in fact, called Goldwater "the Republican Truman."

I have no doubt Barry Goldwater would have made an exceptional president, far exceeding the expectations of both supporters and detractors. His would have been a balanced and positive administration, not ruled by any rigid ideology, and showing great concern for all the people, but especially those struggling to achieve and survive in a sometimes harsh and cruel world.

These words, free from pretense or garnish, sum up Goldwater's persona and his approach to the presidency: "I think of myself as a simple, uncomplicated man. Duty, honor, country hold for me the meaning given them by General Douglas MacArthur. It's not a part of my nature to equivocate. I detest extremism in the presently accepted derogatory connotation of the word. The dictionary gives a number of definitions for *extreme*—'of a character or kind farthest removed from the ordinary or average—the utmost or highest degree.' Those two simple declarative sentences [from his acceptance speech in 1964] summed up my approach to the presidency. For I intended to do my utmost in the defense of liberty and to pursue justice in a manner far removed from the average. . . ."

What more could citizens of a free society expect from their president?

Fate intervened, but I agree with the appraisal by David Nolan in the *Libertarian Party News* that Barry Goldwater was in fact "the greatest president we never had," a leader more effective and influential than many of our presidents.

12

The Days Dwindle Down: Barry on Campaign Finance Reform, Civil Rights, and Nixon's Departure

Life has now come full circle. Today, people want me to give a lot of speeches. I guess some think old Goldwater has finally reached the age of reason.
—BG, 1995

IN THE LAST LONG DECADE of his life after he left the Senate, Barry Goldwater experienced some of his "best" and "worst" years.

There was the good side, the best of times.

Never one to mince words, and a passionate disciple of freedom, Barry found new freedom to say anything he damn well pleased with the Senate behind him. The press seemed, finally, to discover the "real" Goldwater, and he became a newly anointed oracle of wisdom, something of a hero for the candor and good sense that many once ridiculed.

Barry enjoyed loosing thunderbolts from his hilltop home, often with considerable glee, singeing fellow Republicans. He perceived weak leadership and narrowness in his party and ripped with regularity the religious right and others who he often said didn't understand the meaning of the word *conservative*.

Looking back, some more astute and objective members of the fourth estate acknowledged they'd read Barry wrong when he ran for president, and some sought to make amends. When he died in 1998, a writer for *National Review* said some obituaries sounded as if they were meant for Eleanor Roosevelt. Even though he swore he never deviated from his deep-dyed conservative moorings, certain editors and reporters credited him approvingly with a "left turn" and swing into liberalism. When Bob Dole came to visit him at home in Paradise Valley, the two chuckled about their roles as the "new liberals" of the GOP. This was the result of Barry's support of choice for women, for gays in the military and across the board, and his occasional kind words for a Democrat here and there, such as President Bill Clinton ("I think Mr. Clinton is going to be a good president"), Senator Sam Nunn ("one of the most selfless men in the Senate"), and Karan English, who won a seat in Congress with his blessing ("by far the best candidate").

Said Barry, "Life has now come full circle. Today, people want me to give a lot of speeches. I guess some think old Goldwater has finally reached the age of reason. They give me testimonial dinners and hold public ceremonies. Arizona schools, military institutions, roads, and kids are named after me. Defense Secretary Caspar Weinberger, the Joint Chiefs of Staff, and the Pentagon had a big blowout—a seventeen-gun salute, parade, and Air Force flyover. Frankly, there's been too much of this, and I'm glad it's over."

But for Barry, this was the worst, the hardest of times, too. He was acutely conscious of nearing the end. He was in constant, throbbing pain, with a body augmented by spare parts and the surgeon's knife cuts.

"It's not easy coming home," he said, after packing up and taking along the papers, trophies, and memorabilia of thirty years in the Senate.

"I get an odd feeling going out the door knowing my destination is the cactus, the bird feeder, or the hot tub. My early-morning journey these days is tapping my cane along the walk to the tub. A new artificial right knee now eases the ache there—the pain of twenty years finally became too much to bear—but the ache in my left knee lingers. Both came from football and basketball injuries.

"The pain seems to reach everywhere—my heels, shoulders, back, neck, both artificial hips, elbows, chest. A fellow comes to be philosophical about it after more than fifteen operations, including a triple coronary bypass in 1982."

He was lonely and demoralized after Peggy finally succumbed to emphysema and heart problems in late 1985. His relationship with his children was mixed and somewhat distant. He was troubled by their needs for money they thought he should provide. He no longer enjoyed the authority, prestige, and perquisites that came from being a senator. It was a most difficult time.

Things got much better when he married Susan Shaffer Wechsler in February of 1992. Thirty years his junior, she was the attractive, no-nonsense head of

Hospice of the Valley, Arizona's largest such program for the terminally ill. Visitors abounded, boosting his morale, and Susan kept him mostly in good fettle, nudging and cajoling, exuding warmth and affection.

As the days dwindled down, Barry continued outspoken and even more cantankerous than usual until, in September 1996, he was slowed by a small frontal lobe stroke. Susan kept his morale up as best she could, giving him "a kick in the fanny from time to time," and making sure there were friends and other people around to lighten the atmosphere.

Among those who came calling at separate times after Barry's stroke were President Bill Clinton and First Lady Hillary Rodham Clinton, General Colin Powell, and Bob Dole. Goldwater continued to be strong physically, with no paralysis or speech problems, but some memory impairment.

Bill Clinton came to visit in September 1996 while Goldwater was recovering at Barrow Neurological Institute of Saint Joseph's Hospital and Medical Center in Phoenix. The president arrived with his entourage, including White House Chief of Staff Leon Panetta, but insisted on entering Barry's room by himself. Susan said they talked animatedly for an hour and a half on a wide range of subjects. They apparently covered a lot of ground, with Goldwater able to discuss cogently matters of import to both men. They "sat and talked like old friends," she recalled, and they agreed on the importance of accepting homosexuals in the military, "if they could shoot straight," and assuring equal rights for gays in the society at large. Goldwater earlier had won Clinton's gratitude by telling Republicans they should "get off the president's back" on Whitewater, saying, "I haven't heard anything yet that says this is all that big of a deal." Several years earlier, Clinton had appointed Barry to the Comsat board, and Susan remembered the president one day knocked on Goldwater's hotel door to say hello while the retired senator was in Washington for a board meeting.

Hillary came by herself to their Paradise Valley home the next month. Susan said she sat close to Barry's bed and put a hand on his arm as they talked nonstop. Hillary's early affection for the senator was kindled when she and several high school friends became "Goldwater Girls" in 1964, passing out buttons and brochures, in her hometown of Park Ridge, Illinois. She stayed casually in touch and, in a note to me several years ago, referred to "our friend, the irrepressible Barry Goldwater." After her visit, Susan said Barry raved about Hillary's "wonderful coloring" and described her as a "wonderful first lady, independent and strong."

In the half dozen years immediately after he left the Senate, Goldwater paused from time to time to reflect on critical episodes in his life and matters of continuing great import to him. Three stand out in particular.

One "threatening scandal" gnawed at Goldwater: "The sinister influence of money in politics." To the very end, he was greatly disturbed by the corruption of big money. When I visited him at his home in 1994, he told me with feeling: "The role of money is way out of line. It's strangling us. The influence of money distorts everything. Government of and by the people is waning. We may already have gone too far to reverse the role and influence of money in our society." He continued to sound this urgent warning in the years before his death.

Goldwater would have cheered lustily the crusade by his Senate successor, John McCain, to enact tough campaign finance reform. And he would have been

appalled by Texas governor George W. Bush's unprecedented $70 million campaign war chest—meant to
scare off competitors for the Republican presidential
nod—which he mostly spent to overpower McCain in
the primary elections of 2000.

"Hell, we could lick anybody in a war," Goldwater
told me, "but this money thing could topple our democratic system. Too many public officials are bought
and paid for, and the big-money people are increasingly brazen in buying them off. The notion that
restrictions on campaign financing violate First
Amendment rights is so much horse manure. We need
to face up to this money thing. It may be the most dangerous threat we have faced in our 200-plus years as a
free society."

The second event was the unjust charge that he was
racist in his political philosophy. Nothing was more
distressing to Goldwater in his entire life than this.
Everything throughout his life from the earliest days
belied that notion. It was his vote against the historic
Civil Rights Bill of 1964 that gave his foes ammunition
to pursue the racist issue.

"I'll never forget when [Senator Everett] Dirksen
came to my Washington apartment one evening to try

to talk me into voting for the bill. We had a drink, and he talked about history, Lincoln, and the gathering of all of us on the final day of judgment. It was as if he were singing 'Amazing Grace.' I was on the verge of tears. Then he said, 'We need you, Barry. History awaits—but not for long. The river moves on. Time quickens.'"

It was hardly fair. I know from personal experience how convincing old Ev could be.

But Barry clung to his convictions. "I kept nodding yes, yes. Then I came out of his spell and said, 'Hell, no, Ev. Two parts of the bill are unconstitutional. I'm going to vote against them.'" Which he did.

Before casting his vote, he told fellow senators, "I am unalterably opposed to discrimination of any sort, and I believe that though the problem is fundamentally one of heart, some law can help, but not law that embodies features like these, provisions which fly in the face of the Constitution and require for their effective execution the creation of a police state. . . .

"If my vote is misconstrued, let it be, and let me suffer the consequences. My concern extends beyond any single group in our society. My concern is for the entire nation, for the freedom of all who live in it and for all who were born in it. This is my concern, and this is where I stand."

Most of the press called Goldwater a "segregationist." This opinion in *Newsweek* by Walter Lippman shows how far removed from reality was the most venerated journalist of his time in commenting on Goldwater's civil rights stance: "He would nullify if he could the central purpose of the Civil War amendments, and would take from the children of the emancipated slaves the protection of the national union." In other words, restore slavery. It is easy to understand Goldwater's fury and frustration as he read such drivel from esteemed journalists.

A handful defended him. Founder-columnist David Lawrence of *U.S. News* described Goldwater's "no" vote as "the courageous act of a man who would rather risk the loss of a presidential nomination or even an election than to surrender his convictions to political expediency." Arthur Krock of the *New York Times* said Goldwater "set an example of political and moral courage." They were consistent supporters.

Despite his impassioned plea to Barry to support the Civil Rights Act, of which he was "a chief architect,"

Senator Dirksen, in nominating Goldwater at the convention, called his "no" vote an example of "moral courage not excelled anywhere in any parliamentary body of which I have any knowledge."

"Never in my life," Goldwater stated, "had I ever advocated, suggested, or implied any form of racism. Nor, contrary to the repeated claims of various civil rights organizations and [the infamous Scranton letter], had I ever believed in contributing to a 'racial holocaust' by my vote."

Scrutiny of Goldwater's record from his earliest days shows clearly the unfairness of any charge of racism.

Even in his twenties, Goldwater integrated the family stores, and he refused to hold the annual meeting in any hotel that wouldn't admit or serve blacks.

In organizing the Arizona Air National Guard in 1946, Barry "acted alone to provide a desegregated unit." That was before President Truman's desegregation order and nearly two decades before the 1964 Civil Rights Bill. He was a founder of the Urban League in Phoenix. He had long supported the NAACP's campaign to test segregation laws there. In 1990, he endorsed a state proposition to create a paid state holiday honoring Rev. Martin Luther King Jr., even though he had been an outspoken critic of King. In 1994, he received the Civil Libertarian of the Year Award from the Arizona Civil Liberties Union. His friendship with Arizona's minority Native Americans, and their deep-seated affection for him, were almost epic in Arizona.

Downcast by the racist charges that he was forced to endure, Goldwater stated, "Civil rights was a political issue from the start. I became a little sick of the hypocrisy connected with it," which continues apace nationwide today. "I had to vote for every civil rights bill," no matter how flawed or wrongly conceived. "Various people, black and white, wanted the 1964 Act passed for their own ends. This was hard-nosed politics based on self-interest."

Susan Goldwater told me a little story that puts a human face on Barry's attitude toward minorities. A black woman whose daughter worked at the Goldwater store in Phoenix helped in the kitchen at parties in the Goldwater home. After the festivities ended, Barry would go into the kitchen, fix a martini for the weary black maid, and talk with her long into the night.

Nothing made him sadder or angrier than the sniping about his alleged racism, which simply wouldn't stand the hot light of truth.

The third critical episode for Goldwater had to do with Richard Nixon, who was once a good friend and political compatriot but whom Goldwater never completely trusted. In the early stages of Watergate, Goldwater defended Nixon. Then he and Senator Chuck Percy of Illinois called on the president at the White House and urged him to "come clean publicly" on Watergate; they were convinced the people would forgive such an honest disclosure. But Nixon stonewalled, denied knowledge of the break-in, and was unmasked when the tapes were revealed. Goldwater never forgave his onetime associate and branded him a "liar" of the worst type whom he could never again trust or respect.

When the time came, Barry's Senate colleagues unanimously anointed Goldwater to convey to the president that his support had crumbled and he must leave to escape impeachment. Several Republican senators said Goldwater was "the only one blunt enough to get across to Nixon the feeling of most GOP senators."

At first, it was thought Goldwater alone would confront the president. But Nixon wanted Senator Hugh Scott and Congressman John Rhodes, the minority leaders of the Senate and House, to be present, too, so he could get "as broad a picture as possible" on the mood of congressional Republicans.

General Alexander Haig, Nixon's chief adviser, saw Nixon as "a man dancing on the point of a pin. . . . It would be best," said Haig, "not to demand or even suggest that he resign." This might trigger his defiance. Haig said the best thing would be "to show him there was no way out except to quit or lose a long, bitter battle that would be good for no one—the country, Nixon, his family, or the party. The president needs to know there are no more alternatives, no more options."

A little later, ABC reported falsely that Goldwater had said the president would resign, and NBC stated that Goldwater had sought entrance to the White House and been refused. Goldwater was livid.

"I rushed to the floor of the Senate and requested thirty seconds to speak on a point of personal privilege. It was immediately granted. I blew my stack again, stating that both the ABC and NBC stories were completely false. I looked up at the packed press gallery and declared in a loud voice, "You are a rotten bunch!"

Spontaneous applause and cheers ripped through the chamber from visitors in the gallery. Even senators on the floor applauded, Barry said.

It was clear Congress would convict Nixon if there were an impeachment trial. "Haig asked for our assessment. I told him I thought the president would be lucky if he got twelve votes. I said I would not defend the president: I have been deceived by Richard Nixon for the last time. A majority of the Republicans in the Senate share my feelings.

"Knowing his guilt, we couldn't ask our colleagues to vote him innocent. We all were sworn to uphold the Constitution. . . . Loyalty to country transcended loyalty to party. My colleagues commissioned me to call on the president to ask that he resign."

Haig told Goldwater, "The president wanted to do what would be best for the country." "I was in no mood to forgive Nixon for his past actions," Goldwater said, "but I did believe, and I do believe, that in his final hour of agony he was putting the welfare of the nation ahead of every other consideration.

"Haig said the president wanted the three of us—Scott, Rhodes, and myself—to meet with him at the White House. We went there and ultimately were ushered into the Oval Office. When the president received us, he was fresh from having declared he would not resign. He was serene, confident, cheerful. He acted as though he had just shot a hole in one. He put his feet on the desk and talked. I had never seen him so relaxed. He reminisced about the past, recalled how he and I had campaigned together for over twenty years. . . . Almost casually, he asked me how things stood in the Senate. I told him he could count on about twelve votes, possibly as many as fifteen. And that it would take thirty-four to defeat the impeachment charges in the Senate. The other two concurred and added their similar readings. Scott pointed out that a half dozen members of Nixon's administration, including Ehrlichman, Colson, and Dean, had been convicted or pleaded guilty.

"I have always had reservations about Richard Nixon. . . . He always seemed to be too well programmed, to be carefully calculating the ultimate effect of everything he did or said." Goldwater, by contrast, was just the opposite, a politician often accused of "shooting from the lip," of not being prudent or "programmed" at all.

"It is impossible to imagine a greater punishment than this man was preparing to accept," Goldwater said almost mournfully, "to be forced to resign from the nation's highest office—one moment the most powerful, respected leader in the world; the next, disgraced and discredited. The magnitude of the situation brought tears to my eyes. The president knew what he must do. Thank God he did not require us to spell out the message we carried. When we left, he was smiling. Whatever else I may say or think about Richard Nixon, he displayed a quality of courage I have rarely encountered."

Barry Goldwater and his cohorts could truthfully tell the salivating media that they had not called on Nixon to resign, which was the widespread supposition. Goldwater said it occurred to him that "if we had misjudged the president's intentions—if the president didn't resign—our failure to deal bluntly and openly would prove to be a very grievous error. . . . I wondered if judgment had been overruled by emotion."

But that was not to be. At 9 P.M., on the evening of August 8, 1974, Richard Nixon resigned and announced that Vice President Ford would be sworn in as president at noon the following day.

The extent of the trust and respect in which Barry Goldwater was held by his peers in the Senate was affirmed by the mission he had been called on to lead. It was yet further evidence of his pivotal role at the vortex of twentieth-century history.

These were the crucial matters on Barry Goldwater's mind in the final days: the deadly impact of too much money awash in the U.S. political system . . . the distortion of his stand on civil rights and his lifelong support of equal rights for people of every color and race . . . and Richard Nixon's betrayal of the nation by lying about his knowledge of and involvement in Watergate. Still, it was individual liberty, freedom for every man, that mattered most to him. Until his final breath, his beloved country was his first concern.

13

Barry Goldwater Is Gently Laid to Rest in His Beloved Arizona

You are a beautiful man. Your heart is good.
My people will never forget you.
—Tribal Chief Robert Tree
Cody, for Arizona's Native
Americans, at BG's funeral
service, June 3, 1998,
Tempe, Arizona

On June 3, 1998, Barry Morris Goldwater, an American giant of the twentieth century, was gently laid to rest not far from where he was born nearly ninety years earlier, three years before his beloved Arizona was admitted to statehood.

Dignitaries by the dozens, including two planeloads of Senate compatriots, descended on the Arizona State

University campus, but it was the outpouring of ordinary people that reflected even more poignantly the sorrow and trauma felt throughout the entire state and much of the nation as well. It was people from every walk of life, race, and circumstance who made the greatest impact as they filed past his flag-draped casket earlier in the day at the simple, uncathedral-like Trinity Episcopal Cathedral in downtown Phoenix and lined the streets as the somber procession moved slowly past. Everywhere in Arizona, there was sadness over the passing of its favorite son and recognition of his lasting imprint on the ebbing century.

Providing a touch of private levity was Goldwater's daughter Joanne, a resident of Mexico for several years, who said as the funeral cortege crawled through Phoenix, "We decided that we should have the limo pull over so we could get out at a bar and have a shot of tequila. That's what Dad would have done." It didn't happen, of course, but it lightened the family's mood as they advanced slowly toward the funeral service. (That tale comes from Dolores Tropiano's AZBUZZ gossip column in the *Arizona Republic*.)

A two-star Air Force Reserve general, who was addicted to both flight and the military, Barry would have reveled in the pomp of respect and recognition, especially the flyby of F-16 jet fighters in his honor. As the four-ship unit zoomed in over the gathering crowd outside the huge auditorium, one peeled off and shot straight upward into a bright blue sky freckled with thin clouds. The "hole" in the formation traditionally signifies the loss of a fallen airman. Following the twenty-one-gun salute, a solemn honor guard carried his casket onto the stage, and the Thirty-Sixth Army band played a stirring rendition of the national anthem.

Milling about in the foyer outside the capacious Grady Gammage Auditorium was close to one-third of the U.S. Senate and a host of notable friends of the senator. There was Pat Moynihan, tall and teetery. Curmudgeons from the South, ninety-six-year-old Strom Thurmond and ever prickly Jesse Helms. Soon-to-be-departed Newt Gingrich and his counterpart, Senate Majority Leader Trent Lott. Old friends Bob Dole, Dan Quayle, and former U.S. House minority leader John Rhodes of Arizona. Susan Goldwater escorted Nancy Reagan. Former White House chief of staff and retired Senator Howard Baker and Senator Fred Thompson, both Tennesseeans, and then-governor Pete Wilson of

California were on hand. Arizona Governor Jane Hull and five of her predecessors were there, too. It was some of the feeling of "old home week" as the senators and many others, away from their workaday habitats, jovially plied one another with myriad Goldwater stories—funny, warming, grave, bawdy.

The setting was ideal. The Grady Gammage Auditorium, a centerpiece of the Arizona State University campus, was the last major creation of famed architect Frank Lloyd Wright. Barry's ties and commitment to the university were long, deep, and intimate, and his influence there "widespread."

After he left the Senate, "he became a vital part of the ASU community, regularly visiting with students and attending classes . . . providing an extraordinary opportunity for a student to be a part of a historic figure and era," said ASU president Lattie Coor. "He was deeply committed to the goals of the university and of the Goldwater Chair for American Institutions and has been immensely helpful to us as we created that chair as one of the premier positions at ASU."

On this day, a standing-room crowd of more than 3,000, "celebrating" Barry's long, eventful, and illustrious life, jammed the auditorium. The services were conducted by a tandem of clergy: Rabbi Albert Plotkin, reflecting Barry's Jewish heritage on his father's side, and Rev. Carl Carlozzi, an Episcopalian priest representing his mother's religion. Dr. Lloyd Ogilvie, chaplain of the Senate, described Barry's death as "a transition in the midst of living."

On the stage, some of those closest to Barry spoke eloquently.

There was the familiar face of compact, white-haired senior senator John McCain, who later made a strong, principled, Barry-like maverick bid for the Republican presidential nomination in 2000, and who was Goldwater's successor in 1987. He knew Barry well and had his support when he first ran for the seat. His eloquent eulogy included these words:

> Barry served America, all of America, a country conceived in liberty, a country that let you pledge any damn thing you wanted as long as it didn't cost someone else their liberty. He served freedom—a cause greater than, but encompassing, his self-interest—and to that cause he pledged, as a famous group of East Coast radicals once pledged, his life, his fortune, and

his sacred honor. . . . He defended freedom in all its manifestations because he appreciated that freedom conferred on America the distinction of being the last, best hope of humanity, the haven and advocate for all who believed in the God-given dignity of the human being. . . .

Barry Goldwater will always be the senator from Arizona, the one history recalls with appreciation and delight. In all the histories of American politics, he will remain a chapter unto himself. The rest of us will have to make do as footnotes.

There was towering Secretary of the Interior Bruce Babbitt, native Arizonan, former governor, lifelong friend of Barry.

He reminisced about two Arizona icons who are known around the world: "One is Geronimo, and the other is Barry Goldwater. I think that the two of them had many things in common, one of which was a passionate attachment to this land that we love called Arizona. And the other was a passion for freedom and a willingness to defend that freedom."

Then Babbitt read a letter addressed to Susan Goldwater from President Clinton:

Dear Susan:

Hillary and I would wish to be with you, the rest of Barry's family, and the legion of friends from Arizona and the rest of America as you say farewell.

Few Americans in our history have served the people with such a remarkable blend of conviction, integrity, and basic decency.

All of us who knew Barry were lifted by the sparkle in his eyes, the warmth of his heart, the depth of his humanity. He leaves us all the richer for his life and keenly aware of a legacy of citizenship that we must try to emulate.

Now he has taken his best flight, to a better place, which he so richly deserves.

Sincerely,
Bill Clinton

"Barry Goldwater and the Grand Canyon stand together," said Babbitt, "both unique, both monumental, both among the very best of God's creations. I believe that Barry Morris Goldwater will be remembered as long as, each morning, the sun continues to rise over the Grand Canyon."

U.S. Senator John Kyl, Republican from Arizona, said Goldwater "knew, in the end, the most important thing was to tell the truth as he saw it, and to build a foundation for the future." He added: "One reason I think he liked common people is that, like Abraham Lincoln, he saw himself as a common man. . . . There is no doubt that Goldwater—as the path breaker for today's commonsense conservatism—is the most influential Arizonan in our lifetime. . . . There are too few people who give you the feeling that they have the long view in mind. Barry Goldwater did. There are too few who show us what it is like for a man to guide his life by true principles. Barry Goldwater showed us. He was not only a great patriot, he was as he wished to be remembered: a good and honest man."

The unquestioned star of the ceremony was Barry's younger brother, Bob, who regaled the gathering with stories both poignant and hilarious. He gave a sort of affectionate, homespun rendition of "Life with Barry," growing up and over almost nine decades, during which, he told me, they remained "extremely close."

"Our father was Jewish," he said, "but our mother, who came to Arizona from a tiny place in Illinois, was an Episcopalian, and we were brought up Episcopalian, even if Dad didn't like it, because there wasn't a synagogue anywhere to be found back when we were kids.

"Barry was always popular," said his brother. "He was class president at Phoenix Union High School, captain of the teams, a favorite of the girls, but he wasn't a great student. . . . Unfortunately, by the end of the year, instead of having sixteen credits, he had only two. That made Dad pretty unhappy. . . .

"We even had a basketball team. One day Barry came up with a brilliant idea that we should get jerseys and have a big, big letter *P* put on the front of the jersey—*P* for '*Piscopalian*." That brought howls of laughter from the crowd.

"Anyway, after a little talk with the dean, our father told Barry he was going to go to Staunton Military Academy. Barry liked that. It didn't bother him a bit.

"After four years at Staunton [in Virginia], Barry graduated with the highest cadet honors. Now, that didn't include grades or anything, but just being a good cadet—and, of course, the fact that he dated the commandant's daughter might have had something to do with it. . . . Staunton was very good for him. When he graduated, he went to the University of Arizona, where again he was president of the freshman class. He played football, joined the Sigma Chi fraternity, and was just an all-around good boy. But at the end of our freshman year, unfortunately, our father died. And so Barry figured that he should get out of school and come home and run the business, which he did, and he did a good job of it.

"Barry was a real good merchant," said Bob. "Among his innovations was boxer shorts imprinted with red ants and called 'Antsy Pants.' The advertising pitch, dreamed up by Barry: 'You'll rant and dance with ants in your pants.' We ran that ad in *The New Yorker*, and we sold those shorts in every state in the union. It was unbelievable."

Bob told of Barry's idea of printing some of the top branding irons in the state on cloth. "Back in those days, most every store had a piece-goods section because women liked to sew, and so this branding-iron piece good sold all over. . . .

"Barry was a good employer. The employees loved Barry. I don't believe I ever heard anyone in the store call him Mr. Goldwater. It was always Barry, sometimes things a little harsher. Like the time he put what he thought was a dead mouse in one of those pneumatic tubes and sent it up to accounting. It bounced down in front of our cashier, Clara Mains, and when she emptied the container, the mouse suddenly came to life, and she chased Barry all over the store screaming when she recovered from her shock.

"We should also tell you that we have a sister, Carolyn [she died about a year after Barry did], who did a lot in shaping Barry's life, and he did a lot in shaping hers. He told her that if a boy kissed her, she'd get pregnant."

Bob spoke about Barry's cornucopia of hobbies and diversions beyond politics. He gave a kind of Norman Rockwell tableau of their life growing up. It would have made several nostalgic *Saturday Evening Post* covers.

"We had a big vacant lot next door. Barry played pretty good baseball [as a kid]. . . . He batted cross-hand, but he was still a pretty good hitter.

"Our mother would take us out to the Indian School. They had a band, and the band played every night, and they had a band shell, and they took the flag down every night, and they would play a retreat. It added to

Barry's sense of patriotism. I guess you might say he's always been very particular about the new flag and how it should be handled, and of course he got a lot of that growing up.

"He was a ham radio operator, and he had a group of ham radio operators in Phoenix. They ran the radio station at our house twenty-four hours a day so these soldiers over in Vietnam could get into an army station and send a message home. Barry worked out a deal with AT&T where he got a special rate and hooked these kids up with their parents or their wives. And they did over 300,000 patches. Now, that's really dedication, and till this day he had people call him on the ham radio just to want to talk. And they thought it was great. . . .

"You all have seen his photographs, and they were beautiful. Those are things he worked on as he was growing up, and I think it sort of molded his character, and he got it in pretty good shape.

"We also had a soda pop stand out in front of the house. We could buy soda pop for three cents a bottle, and we just had a couple of wooden boxes out on Central Avenue. We got the ice out of the house for nothing. We didn't pay any rent, had no electric bill. We sold it for five cents so we were making two cents a bottle. That's pretty good, and we didn't pay any taxes." The early Goldwater entrepreneurial instinct.

The audience paid rapt attention as Bob continued to sketch out his intimate eulogy to his big brother.

"Dad couldn't drive, but my mother could, and we would go up to the Indian country, and we saw things like the Snake Dance. All of those things helped form Barry's life. That's where he got the love for the Indians, now called the Native Americans.

"We also used to go to the beaches out in Los Angeles, Santa Monica, Venice, and believe it or not, some trips would take us four days to drive over there. We'd put the cots on the running boards, and we had to have a lot of water to drive over there. It wasn't just for yourself to drink. It was for the cars. The radiators weren't worth a damn. But all of those things, I think they all helped Barry become what he was.

"He was a nut on flying. He went out to Luke Air Force Base and asked them if they needed any help, and after a lot of maneuvering around, they let him in as an infantry officer. But then through his photography he would bribe pilots by telling them to take him up and give him a little stick time, and he'd take their picture flying, and they could have these pictures to send home, and sure, they're glad to do that. And after a time, why, he went to the commandant and asked for an exam. He said he thought he was capable of flying; he'd been flying the AT6 trainers. The guy gave him an exam, and Barry got his wings. I don't think anybody else ever got wings like that, but Barry was a rather unusual character.

"I believe it was Everett Dirksen who nominated Barry for president at the convention in San Francisco. And the way he did it, he said he wanted to nominate a peddler's grandson. That was my grandfather who started the store. . . . Anyways, I bet Everett Dirksen would be proud of Barry today, and I bet the old peddler would be proud of him, too.

"I know if he hasn't already, he'll be seeing his father and mother soon, and they'll be proud of him. And Carolyn and I are proud of him. God bless you."

Bob retreated to his seat on the stage to a standing ovation from the mourners, whom he had charmed with his warm stories.

Near the end, Native American chief Robert Tree Cody, dressed in colorful tribal regalia, played a flute solo and, in a sonorous tone, uttered these words: "You are a beautiful man. You are a great man. Your heart is good. You are with the elders now. You are a chief. My people will never forget you."

Finally, Barry Jr., former congressman from California, walked to the casket in the center of the stage and promised his father, "The Goldwater legacy will continue. Happy trails, Dad." And a member of the Air Force honor guard presented the folded flag to Susan, Barry's lovely widow.

AFTERWORD

Farewell to a Friend

HILLARY RODHAM CLINTON[1]

I first met Barry Goldwater during the 1964 presidential campaign. My best friend, Betsy, and I were "Goldwater Girls." We wore cowboy hats and red, white, and blue sashes anchored by gold buttons reading AuH_2O. At the end of a long, tiring day, the senator politely shook hands with all the workers there, including the teenagers like myself. This is the Barry Goldwater I think of so often.

I supported Barry Goldwater in 1964 partly because my father was a committed Republican (that is, until he met Bill Clinton). But what really won me over was the senator's book, *Conscience of a Conservative*. I volunteered in August 1964—my first foray into presidential politics. I was hooked on the importance—and fun—of citizen involvement in our nation's politics. Later, as

Reprinted by permission of Creators Syndicate.

my political beliefs evolved, they didn't always match the senator's. But they remained rooted in the same commitment to American leadership and individual responsibility. I knew his politics were honestly derived and based on his patriotism and sense of fair play. Despite our political differences, my admiration for him never waned. We shared a deep love of country and, over time, we found ourselves once again agreeing on some things—including the hot peppers, salsa, and chili he made sure I had plenty of in the White House.

The last time I saw him was during a visit to his home in Paradise Valley on October 15, 1996. Sharing time with him and his wife, Susan, gave me a keener sense of the man. I found him as outspoken and plain-spoken as ever. I renewed the president's invitation for him to ride on Air Force One, which he had helped design, and he promised he would when he felt well enough. Regrettably, that day never came.

I, along with Americans everywhere, salute Barry Goldwater and thank him for a lifetime of dedication to our country, which he loved so much.

Index